PRECISION SELLING

JOSEPH S. LAIPPLE

PRECISION SELLING

A GUIDE FOR COACHING SALES PROFESSIONALS

PMP

Performance Management Publications (PMP)
3353 Peachtree Road NE, Suite 920
Atlanta, Georgia 30326
1.800.223.6191

Performance Management Publications (PMP)

3353 Peachtree Road NE, Suite 920

Atlanta, Georgia 30326

1.800.223.6191

International Standard Book Number: 0-937100-12-9

Printed in the United States of America

05   04   03   02   01

Cover and text design by Lisa Smith

PMP books are available at special discounts for bulk purchases by corporations, institutions, and other organizations. For more information, please call 678.904.6140, extension 131, or e-mail lglass@aubreydaniels.com.

PRECISION SELLING

Precision Selling offers a sensible solution to the sales equation. Joe Laipple has captured a direct, practical approach to selling using sound principles and methods. This book will absolutely assist anyone who is trying to master the art of sales!

–Brian K. Mossor
Vice President,
Leadership, Technology & Professional Development
Comcast Cable Communications

Precision Selling sorts through the complex world of sales and focuses on behaviors that make a difference. The author provides a concise roadmap for optimizing sales results. Anyone interested in improving the effectiveness of their sales team should apply these principles.

–Tom Klein
Senior Executive,
Pharmaceutical Industry

I will boldly state that this is the most important sales coaching book ever written because it describes the specific actions that sales leaders must take to influence salespeople to succeed. Also, the *Key Actions* at the end of each chapter make this a quick and easy-to-use guide to make great sales happen.

–Mark S. Repkin
Vice President
The Certif-A-Gift Company

Great book! *Precision Selling* provides a step-by-step process for improving the discretionary performance of any sales team. I highly recommend it!

–Gino F. Cozza
Managing Director
Chrysler Financial Canada

Sales leaders will recognize themselves as they digest this compelling and practical guide to effective sales practices. Laipple skillfully distills the challenges that even the most successful teams face and describes effective, doable methods to get your team to the next level. This book is a must read for sales leaders in any business.

–Steve Sherline
Affiliate Sales Manager
Fifth Third Securities, Inc.

ACKNOWLEDGMENTS

I probably have about ten drafts of various book ideas and outlines buried somewhere on my computer that would remain mere concepts for potential books if it were not for people who have encouraged me to write beyond the outline. I needed people checking in, following up, describing the potential impact that writing the book might have on my work, and telling me how helpful it could be for my current and future clients. In short, I needed consequences to shape my behavior as a writer. I would like to thank those individuals who supported me throughout the writing process.

First, I'd like to thank my wife Mary Laipple for encouraging me to take the time to sit down, write, and rewrite the various drafts of the book. Your support and encouragement have helped me more than I can say.

Aubrey Daniels kindly asked me to write the first outline of this book and e-mail it to him. After I did that, he asked me to start writing chapter one. He soon asked me how that was going. I think your prompts and follow-up helped me jump-start this entire process. I'd also like to acknowledge that this book would not be possible had you not written your books: *Performance Management, Bringing Out the Best in People, Other People's Habits,* and *Measure of a Leader. Precision Selling* is a specific application of the behavioral science you have described so well.

My thanks to

Darnell Lattal who has not only encouraged me to write about Precision Selling but has also been supportive to me personally and professionally.

Gail Snyder for your practical advice and careful editing. You have continually helped me to write plainly and clearly.

Brenda Jernigan for your keen review of previous drafts. You helped me remove some of the clutter that was in previous drafts.

Laura Lee Glass for guiding this book through the maze that is the publishing process.

Lisa Smith for your quick and practical help in graphic design. I knew that I was in good hands with every version of the original covers.

Mark Repkin, an exceptional salesperson and sales coach, for providing practical and essential feedback on earlier drafts of the manuscript, support throughout the entire writing process, and for taking the time to help me come up with a title that I like.

Deb Brucker, Gino Cozza, Paul Dempsey, Tom Klein, Brian Mossor, Charlie Mustachia, Tony Pangi, Steve Sherline, Tom Spencer, Julie Terling, and Rose Vitale for comments on earlier drafts and the cover.

John Green, who is a superlative coach of sales leaders and who has an uncanny ability to translate behavioral science to the real world. He has been a co-creator of how these methods can be applied to sales and service organizations and how to do it in a way that gets to the point quickly. Through his practice, he has also revealed and emphasized the pragmatic and contextual elements within applied behavioral science.

Finally, I'd like to thank my father, Bill Laipple, for letting me tag along when you made sales calls. You taught me to be a good observer, what it takes to sell well, and how to coach good sales performance. You remain peerless in the way you influence others.

TABLE OF CONTENTS

PREFACE

*The difference between winners and losers is that winners
do things losers are not willing to do.*

Anonymous

A lot of work, extra effort, and a little luck go into the big sale. The primary challenge is that big sales don't occur often enough to inspire even effective salespeople to do the right things all the time. Salespeople do a lot of the right things each day; yet often either their efforts have no impact or their customers give them negative reactions anyway. So what do salespeople need to do when good things don't happen each time they do the right things? What do salespeople do as they work toward the big sale? How do they keep engaged in the right things, right now—today—when they know it will take time for their hard work to pay off? If you are a sales coach, how *do* you actually help your salespeople do the right things that lead to sales?

The goal of this book is to help sales coaches do more of the right activities that *help* their salespeople improve sales. Precision Coaching is about identifying and engaging in specific coaching actions that are required to help improve sales. It is about helping your salespeople sell more effectively by applying proven behavioral science to sales—something called Precision Selling. Effective selling and coaching require focusing on the basics, the fundamentals, the essentials. In fact, I don't think easy answers to the challenges of sales and sales coaching exist. Precision Coaching is about how to do the things that we know we *should* do, but for some reason don't do on a *consistent* and *constant* basis. Once we understand the reasons why we do some things versus others and why we don't always do the things that we are supposed to do (even when we know those things are good for us), then we can begin to improve our own performance as well as the performance of others.

Let's face it. The real world gets in the way of effective selling habits, effective training, and good intentions. Precision Coaching, as described here, is designed to help you recognize and counteract those real-world barriers to success. It is also designed to help salespeople focus on the right things that lead to the right kind of sale over the long term: I call it Precision Selling. Precision Coaching uses the science of human behavior to improve how you coach others to sell. My interest and experience in sales, however, did not start with science. It started with observing a consummate salesperson in action—my father.

From my father, I learned firsthand about the joys, pleasures, and challenges of selling. When I was a kid, he was a tire salesman for various companies in Buffalo, New York, and at times his territory covered most or all of New York state and portions of Western Pennsylvania. My dad provided my first example of just what a salesperson is and what selling is all about. I often accompanied him on sales trips and during the summer, he sometimes asked me if I wanted to go with him for the week. I jumped at the chance, primarily because I enjoyed driving around, seeing new places, eating at diners and restaurants, staying at a motel, and especially talking to my dad.

On Sunday night, I prepared for the trip by looking at a map to find the places we would be going and packing my bag with clothes, a few comic books, and a novel or other reading material. I'd attempt to get to bed early, because I knew we'd be leaving almost at the break of dawn. Monday morning finally arrived and we'd be on our way, hitting the road early enough to be at the customer location just when it opened. We'd also get up early enough to enjoy breakfast near the customer site as my dad prepared for his sales visit. He might review customer data or check on whether the customer got the products and service he wanted the last time he was there. He often told me details about his customers, and described their personalities down to their specific likes and dislikes. He knew his customers well and at times had breakfast, lunch, or dinner with them.

When he sold, he was as much a customer advocate as a salesperson. He knew the customers and knew what they needed to run their businesses effectively. I got the sense that he really worked for his customers rather than any company he happened to have on his business card. I suspect his bosses thought his customers had more influence on him than *they* did. If they did think so, they were right.

Sometimes, I'd just sit in the car and listen to the radio, read, or walk around outside while my dad met with his clients. Most of the time though I'd walk right in there with him and meet his customers. My dad taught me to address customers with the appropriate greeting (always Mr., Miss, or Mrs.), offer a firm handshake, look them in the eye, and say something such as, "Good to meet you" or "Nice to see you again." Then I'd sit quietly, listen to my dad talk to them, and watch how they treated my dad. We'd often meet with the owners of the company. During those days, the business owners were primarily men and they usually did it all—ran the business, repaired and drove their company trucks, and managed their people. These visits taught me that how well you dress, how you talk, how you look, and how clean your hands are doesn't really tell much about how successful you are in your life. My dad knew his customers' names, their kids' names, their spouses' names, and many of the other workers' names. Occasionally, I'd meet them too.

I enjoyed these visits. The people were nice and I learned a lot just by observing and listening. I often wondered when my father was actually selling. I guess it was when he pulled out his pricing sheets or when they talked about how many or the type of tires the customer wanted to buy. But I don't think they bought from my father because he had the best price or the perfect tire. It was something else. He asked a lot of questions. He listened and he followed up. If his customers didn't receive the product or service they needed or that he had promised, Dad followed through to make sure they did get what he promised, and when they needed it.

At other times, my father looked for new business from people he didn't know at all or didn't know well. Sometimes I'd go on these visits too, but they were different. My dad described some of these potential customers as tough and, as a young kid, I was a little wary of these people. But then I saw my dad, smiling just like he did with the guys who liked him, and talking toe-to-toe, just like he did with those other guys.

I particularly remember my dad telling me about one man whom I imagined as a scary person. Surprisingly, Dad always smiled as he told me about encounters with this tough man, who was going to eventually say yes. He'd been saying no to my father for many months. But he wasn't just saying no; he was throwing him out! As a kid, I found this embarrassing. My father was getting thrown out and he was smiling about it. "Why don't you just stop visiting this guy?" I'd ask.

"I want his business and someday, I'll get it," he answered. "All I need is to get a little bit of business with him. Once I do, I have a shot at getting more business."

Over the course of a few months, this trucking business owner said the following to my dad: "No, I don't want your business." "No, get off my property." "No, I already have a tire guy." "No, I don't need what you're selling." "Don't you understand? No. Get outta here." "No, I said, no. Do you know the meaning of no?"

Then one day my dad walked in with his sales packet and that unflappable smile to see this man yet again and this time he didn't get a no. He got a bewildered look from his future customer and then laughter. The tough guy said, "What do I have to do to get you to stop bothering me?"

"Buy some of my tires," my dad answered.

And he did. This initial small sale led to larger and larger sales. All of those sales included effective follow-up skills and Dad earned the right to future sales. Eventually, this tough guy became one of my dad's best customers.

This experience taught me several lessons:

- No isn't necessarily bad. It doesn't mean no for eternity.

- You don't have to accept no from a customer, at least not over the long term.

- You can work through the nos to earn a yes.

- Getting resistance doesn't mean you should give up.

- Resistance is a test. It happens to us all. How you respond when someone says, "You can't," "You shouldn't," "You won't" makes a difference in the outcome.

- No is only a response. It can be a beginning just as easily as it can be an ending.

My father's response to the no is worth examining in more detail because within that example reside some answers to how to sell and how to help people who are trying to sell. The key to effective sales-manship is not all about the revenue one generates. The answers are not all about the glory of the big sale, but about the little things that a salesperson can do on a regular basis to influence a buyer and build good business over the long run. One reality is common to most sales situations: salespeople hear *no* more often than they hear *yes* during the average sales day. So how do they continue selling despite hearing what they don't want to hear from the customer and how do they then recognize opportunities in a no? How do they get the customer to say yes or shape customers from their current state to another state closer to the sale?

In many sales environments, the customers are the people who actually manage salespeople—this observation is often met by sales coaches with initial disagreement but then begrudging acknowledgment. Salespeople typically see or talk to customers more often than they talk to their sales coaches. In some organizations, salespeople may only see their bosses in the field once every two to three months, if ever. The kind of customers they see also makes a difference in the kind of salesperson they might become. Many salespeople call on the easy customers, the ones who will say yes but who may not provide them with much business. They may take the nos and move on and say, "I've tried my best with those customers, but they're not going to buy anything from me." They may make quick calls to get in their daily or weekly sales call numbers to avoid trouble with their bosses. This is especially true when their bosses spend too much time just looking at the number of sales calls the salespeople make rather than what they do when they make those sales calls. They may make sales calls quickly to avoid a burden on their customers, or so they can get to other things that are more interesting and easier than actually selling.

Are sales coaches letting the no from difficult customers influence their salespeople to take the path of least resistance? Are salespeople responding to the customer's actions in the moment and not pushing back in an effective way? Effective selling is not all nice stuff. It requires being direct, asking productive questions, and sometimes even disagreeing with your customers in the right way. Of course, the nos could help you decide how to best spend your time, but a no is not necessarily a stop sign.

My father somehow was shaped by his environment to engage in certain sales behaviors despite the frequent and inevitable rejections that so frequently occur for salespeople. How do you create this kind of resilience so that your salespeople continue to press for the sale, despite the nos from potential customers? The task of the sales coach is to develop individuals who sell despite the challenges presented by typical customers. One of the primary outcomes of this book is to show sales coaches how to help salespeople focus with precision on the activities within their control that can optimize their sales and enable them to develop long-term, positive customer relationships.

My father is one of the most optimistic people I've ever met, and any discussion with him leaves you feeling like you can accomplish anything. During his sales career, he possessed a strange kind of optimism reflecting not naïveté, nor false promises, but a humble acknowledgment that he would worry about only those things he could control and not worry about those things he could not control. And then he worked on those things he could control to create the best possible outcome. This seems to be the challenge of many sales coaches: how do you help salespeople focus on the right things in their everyday sales, even when those right things are tough to do and may not pay off immediately or every time?

I feel fortunate to have observed this salesperson in action and for the opportunity to learn from him. I had a first-rate role model and sales coach then and now as I think about how to sell and how to improve how I sell. My father raised three boys who know how to sell in their respective fields because he was not only a salesman, he was a sales *coach* to me and my brothers, Mike and Bill. We learned life lessons from him that have helped all three of us work with our customers in a way that brings results beyond just having people say, "Yes, I will buy that." All three of us have a history of long-term customers who have found value not only in the product or service we were selling but in the value and follow-up they receive when buying from us. The lessons from my father combined with my experience and training in behavioral science and my experience as a salesperson, sales coach, and sales consultant form the foundation of this book.

Precision Selling, the specific selling process as described in this book, and Precision Coaching, the specific coaching process described here, have a longer history than my early boyhood sales trips. Both are based on behavioral science, more than seventy years of laboratory research, and thirty-plus years of field application in a myriad of organizations. This science was translated for the general business community most notably by Aubrey C. Daniels (1993; 2003; 2005). Daniels' writings provide further detailed descriptions of the science of human behavior, discretionary effort, the effects of consequences, and so on. I encourage readers interested in more details on the science behind Precision Selling and Precision Coaching to start with the book *Bringing Out the Best in People* (Daniels 1993).

The following chapters provide help to sales coaches who want to focus their efforts precisely on the things that help them influence their salespeople in their day-to-day selling. The work of the sales coach is primarily Precision Coaching. The work they are attempting to influence is not selling in general, but very specific kinds of selling activities. The focus here is about providing not only a description of the science behind Precision Selling and Precision Coaching, but also instructions for how these methods can be applied most effectively. Real-life examples are also provided that salespeople may find are similar to the situations they face with their customers.

CHAPTER ONE

PROFITABLE SALES

Money. You know what that is, the stuff you never have enough of, little green things with George Washington's picture that men slave for, commit crimes for, die for. It's the stuff that has caused more trouble in the world than anything else we ever invented, simply because there's too little of it.

From the film noir classic, *Detour* (1945)

Symptom—Most sales coaches were once very successful salespeople. When asked to improve sales results, sales coaches initially may try to help by trying their own version of coaching. When results don't improve immediately, they may try to help their sales team by selling with them. Have you wondered how you can really optimize the sales results of your team through targeted coaching?

Remedy—This chapter shows how you can use sales coaching to optimize how your salespeople sell, so that they improve their sales numbers. The best kind of sales coaching improves sales results, not just the selling activity.

Let's start by identifying the end result that salespeople want—*a profitable sale*. Precision Selling is about crafting what salespeople do on a daily, weekly, and monthly basis that produces the desired result. The primary desired result may be more than a profitable sale. It could be other results such as long-term customer relations, customer profiling for future sales, delivering services that lead to future sales, customer retention, market penetration, and protecting market share. Precision Selling includes the problem-solving technique of working backward from the final goal to help determine the specific steps required to achieve desired results.

Working backward means first helping salespeople clearly identify the results they really do want. In one company I worked with, for example, the sales leaders initially encouraged their people to call on more customers. The sales leaders were pleased when the sales force increased customer contacts but were surprised that the amount of sales did not increase. Upon further examination, they discovered that the salespeople were calling on more of the convenient-to-see customers who were not among those customers who frequently bought from this organization. In another organization, sales leaders who wanted their salespeople to increase the volume of their sales were happy that the volume of the sales increased but were surprised that they were still losing money at the organizational level because salespeople were lowering prices to improve their volume numbers. The leaders who made these requests and set these directions were later heard saying, "I guess they gave me what I asked for, but that's not what I meant."

I've also heard leaders say in response to these examples, "That's right; you get what you measure." But that's not completely right either. Organizations measure many things and typically use hundreds, perhaps thousands, of measures. The *critical* measures are those measures that leaders follow up on. The few measures that leaders follow up on are the measures that employees typically pay attention to.

The real issue is not only to measure, but rather to be careful of the activities and results you follow up on, recognize, and reward—because you *will* get more of those activities and results. If we ask people to do something, and then we measure it and follow up, we usually get that something again even if it's not the right something. Often, the behaviors and results that leaders ask for are not really the ones that they want. For example, leaders often ask for things that are easy or convenient to measure and then follow up on those things. Smart employees figure this out and give leadership what it thinks it wants—they complete the paperwork, give the boss the numbers they are looking for, tell the boss what he/she wants to hear—and they give just enough so that they don't have to hear about it later. This is one of the central methods of running organizations, and successful employees figure it out quickly.

It's the Same Ballpark

As described in Michael Lewis's (2003) book, *Moneyball,* it is important to focus on the right measures when building a winning baseball team, especially when you can't afford to buy the best players. Lewis's book describes how, using decades of historical data, the Oakland A's clearly defined the kinds of players they should get on their team by studying the statistics that were correlated with a team's winning percentage. The answer they discovered was different from how baseball historically defines best players. Historically, professional baseball organizations have based decisions of *best* based on a player's statistics, baseball folklore, perception, and scouting tradition. Lewis describes how Billy Beane and the Oakland A's, despite a lean payroll, remained competitive by focusing on unique measures of success (measures that, until recently, others have overlooked). They focused on measures that appear to correlate with winning percentage based on extensive statistical analyses. Billy Beane focused on players who extended the inning through walks, hits, and getting hit.

The short answer is to select the right players based on the right kind of results measures. For example, batters who found ways to get on base with hits and walks and who stayed on base longer (those who successfully stole bases or avoided outs with smart base running) added more value than those who had higher batting averages but who rarely got on base through walks and who were often called out as they ran bases.

The relevant lesson in *Moneyball* for sales coaches is to identify and focus precisely on the critical few, right results measures that lead to sustainable long-term success. This is required even if it goes against history, tradition, convention, and the politics of organizations. This approach can help leaders offer clear direction to best influence current players. This method could also be used to select and hire future exceptional players. It is not just a matter of selecting the right people, but also regularly evaluating success, determined not necessarily by the typical standards but by recently discovered standards of success.

Whether you agree or disagree with the statistics and measures described in *Moneyball,* the book highlights a way of improving performance using a *systematic, data-based* approach that can be repeated and that can give the edge to those using it. Several teams in the 2004 and 2005 baseball seasons used this method, including the A's, the LA Dodgers, the Boston Red Sox, and the Houston Astros. In the 2004 season, the Red Sox used this precise, disciplined, data-based approach for running a baseball team to counteract years of a so-called curse, marked by many seasons of bad luck. They went on to win the World Series and as a long-time Yankees fan, I am reluctantly making this point.

Another lesson is *don't use every measure just because you have it and have always done it that way.* Many of those who run baseball organizations still focus on common sense and folklore to define talent, rather than looking at the objective data that really define good baseball players. "He looks like a good baseball player" may not be the best way to recruit baseball players (or salespeople). It's also not the most effective way to run any kind of organization.

Winning Over the Long Term

Who are the best salespeople in an organization? I've asked sales coaches (supervisors of salespeople) and sales leaders (those who lead sales organizations and/or have sales coaches reporting to them) to answer this question. They tell me that the best salespeople are those who do well year after year. These people may not always be Number One, but their sales results are almost always in the top third of the sales organization. These salespeople get the most that is possible out of a given territory or with products that are good and not so good. These salespeople succeed in top territories and they succeed when they are dropped into struggling territories. These salespeople figure it out, and they don't sit around and let the bad results pile up. They bring in help when they need it, and they proactively use data to make a case when their efforts aren't successful. Salespeople who are successful over time focus on the history that matters and use the right historical data, if it is available.

Organizations feel lucky when they have salespeople like this. Of course, one approach is to hire as many salespeople like this as possible. However, since the sales coaching method described here is repeatable, why not do the things that help every person on your team become this type of salesperson? Why not help yourself sell in a way that gets the most out of every situation? Why not perform the best that is possible year after year? If you are a leader, why not help your salespeople optimize their results by focusing on the right behaviors that actually help them, rather than grasping at straws and driving them crazy with requests that may hinder their success?

The first step is to determine the activities that lead to the desired result—a sale. The consistent activities of the performers (sellers) as well as those who coach, develop, support, and hire them (sales leaders and coaches) are critical to achieving consistent and profitable results. We can fill the day completing mountains of reports, calling on easy-to-see customers, trying to put out fires, collecting data and information, and doggedly following company tradition or we can spend the day doing the precise activities that most efficiently and effectively help us reach the desired result over the long term. We can fill the day doing busywork or we can fill the day doing just enough of the right activities to keep us on track and to capitalize on the potential for sustained growth. Precision Coaching and Precision Selling, in short, require us *to clearly and accurately define the key results that we want and then to define the activities (behaviors) that help us get those key results.*

We start then with the results that sellers and sales coaches want. What do you want when it comes to sales results? The easy answer is a sale. But are there other results that sales coaches, sales managers, and sales organizations want from their salespeople? Of course. Legitimate results may help successful salespeople stay on track each day so that, over time, they will be successful. Valued results, other than increasing revenue, might be related to your customers—influencing customers, getting customers to say yes, forming relationships with customers that lead to future sales, gaining access to certain customers, eliciting specific decisions from customers, or spending more time with them. Focusing on customer behaviors is often the reason that good salespeople become great salespeople.

Precision Selling is the way to build science into your sales coaching. Good salespeople figure out the science by reading the right cues in their customers and responding appropriately. This is not usually something they are taught; they learn it through experience and, more often than not, through a time-consuming, trial-and-error approach. Still, when asked about how they do what they do, they often struggle to tell you how or why. This struggle might be because they are so fluent at selling that they can't explain how they do it. But I think there is another influencing factor here. Great salespeople know that this information is their competitive advantage and are often unwilling to share it with others. A lack of sharing best practices is common within sales organizations, especially in those where rankings are used. Rankings (first, second, third and so on) provide reasons for salespeople to keep their best practices to themselves. *Rankings often serve as a natural roadblock to the sharing of best practices since a peer's improved performance threatens one's own ranking.* Sales managers and coaches should work on creating systems that don't rank performers, but instead encourage or reward them for sharing best practices with one another—the possibility of a bonus or reward (in addition to individual sales commission) for overall group performance, for example.

Managing Consequences

Sometimes people act in certain ways on the job for not-so-obvious reasons. We may do things that we think will result in consequences we want, such as keeping the boss off our backs, retaining our jobs, or possibly getting promoted. These perceived or real outcomes are often cited by salespeople as some of the reasons they do what they do (or don't do what they are supposed to do). It is important for sales coaches to understand the impact that these kinds of outcomes might have on overall performance. For example, many salespeople feel particularly challenged when they are asked to do things that take them away from selling. I've known salespeople who spend a great deal of time getting their reporting just right so that they can show the boss the kind of job they are doing.

These same salespeople could have made two more customer calls instead and still have provided adequate but less detailed reporting to their boss. But if the boss is making a big deal about how nice and thorough certain people's reports are, he could be sending a mixed message to the rest of the team. That is, it's not really about selling, it's mainly about giving me the information that I requested so that I look good to my boss who may be recognizing me for those things because it pleases his boss, and so on all the way to the top of the corporate ladder.

Consequences that occur every day can make or break performance. Positive consequences can range from the personal—autonomy, more time off, or beating the competition—to those that are clearly related to financial gain such as a future sale, a future bonus, or winning a trip or contest. Each of these consequences could be used to help salespeople and sales coaches manage their activities in a successful way.

Results, Leading Indicators, and Behaviors

Results that occur later in time (such as market share, volume, positive customer relations) are sometime referred to as **lagging results,** since there is a lag in time between daily activities and results. Salespeople might have to do hundreds of things over many days to establish a positive relationship with a customer, for instance. Salespeople might have several conversations with customers to get them to say yes. These conversations occur over the course of days, weeks, and months, and the sale lags behind the many activities that bring about the sale. In addition to market share, volume, and positive customer relations, other typical lagging results include things like market share change, volume change, customer loyalty, customer retention, and even employee retention and enhanced culture. Each of these lagging results occurs as a result of behaviors, over time, and cannot be accurately measured in the short term. These are the kinds of results that are typically reviewed on a monthly, quarterly, or yearly basis.

Organizations, sales leaders, and sales coaches may attempt to react to poor lagging results with fire drills, special projects, and detailed analyses. Often just refocusing on effective daily practices will right the ship and improve the results over the long term. The challenge here is that firefighting and special projects produce a feeling, perception, and impression of at least doing something NOW. But these efforts often do not improve the situation over time. They often only provide the appearance of an effort to do something so that anyone watching can feel assured that the problem is at least being addressed. Often problems just go away. Perhaps this is due to other factors beyond the control of the organization, the sales coaches, and salespeople (factors like market trends, business cycles, and seasonality).

Other results called **leading indicators** occur right now as we are waiting to see what happens with the lagging results. Leading indicators occur close in time to the behaviors and activities that lead to sales. Leading indicators precede and predict lagging results. They are also the indicators that most closely follow everyday activities and therefore most strongly influence the behaviors of salespeople. Typical leading indicators include access to customers, the amount of time with customers, or customer commitments that might be a yes or a decision from the customer, whether that is an agreement to buy or agreement to let the salesperson provide more information/detail, to answer a specific question, or to meet again in the future.

The concepts of leading indicators and lagging results are important for sales coaches to understand and use to help guide sales activity. Continued focus only on the lagging results could drive erratic sales behavior and activity rather than precise, effective, and efficient sales behavior. A focus only on lagging results also steers the sales manager's efforts toward micromanagement and compliance issues (administrative activities, for example, rather than critical sales activities). Efforts should be focused on creating more of the leading indicators that, over time, produce the lagging results and on the sales and sales coaching behaviors that produce *both* desired leading indicators and lagging, continuous results.

The process of working backward from the desired result helps us focus on what is necessary to do to get what we want. Working backward helps us avoid the traps created by our current habits and guides us toward the critical behaviors that employees at all levels must demonstrate to satisfy their customers. This exercise links the behaviors of leaders, coaches, and sellers to customer needs and key business results. The point is to clearly define the behaviors (for each group) that are likely to have the biggest impact. Organizations can use the process flow summarized in the graphic on the following page to target the critical behaviors within each job that impact sales results.

LINKING SALES BEHAVIOR TO RESULTS

This chapter provided an overview of the lagging results and leading indicators that salespeople and sales organizations typically focus on as they attempt to improve performance. Precision Selling provides a scientific basis for clearly linking leading indicators (which are the results of the *behavior* of salespeople and sales coaches) to lagging results. The next chapter provides an overview of how to link behaviors to leading indicators.

Key Actions Ensure that any coaching and change effort is firmly grounded in achieving an enduring, strategically important business result. Clearly define the leading indicators and lagging results that you want prior to initiating coaching activities.

CHAPTER TWO

SELLING WITH PRECISION

Science may be described as the art of systematic oversimplification.

Karl Popper

...every genuine imaginative act begins down there, with the facts, with the specific, and not with the philosophical, the ideological, or the abstract.

Philip Roth

Symptom—Are your salespeople being managed more by their customers than by you? Do they spend more time with their customers than with you? Do they indicate that they are less likely to try new things because of how they think the customer will respond?

Remedy—This chapter provides an introduction to building customer behavior into your coaching so the customers can work for you while you attempt to provide helpful coaching. It describes how to get past wishing, hoping, and waiting to build effective behavioral methods into your coaching.

11

Precision Selling is a process of working from the long-term as well as the short-term outcomes you desire and then identifying behaviors that help you get there. This includes the behaviors of salespeople as well as the behaviors of customers. The word *behavior* has taken on a wide range of meanings over the last twenty-five years. I will be using a precise, technical definition of that word in this book: *behavior* as used here refers essentially to what people *say* and *do*. Clearly described behaviors are stated objectively. A more detailed description of behavior is provided in the chapter on pinpointing.

The more common use of the word *behavior* has some connotations that are not helpful here. The word *behavior* may present a challenge because it is often used in the context of bad behavior. In terms of sales, the distinction is whether the behavior is desirable (it helps you achieve what you intend to achieve) or undesirable (it does not have the intended impact). Also, please note, the assumption here is that all recommended sales behaviors fall under the category of *ethical sales conduct. Behavior* might also be used as a general term referring to any action (such as listening or questioning). Behavior in many organizations has become synonymous with people, the soft stuff, or the stuff other than the results. In that usage, behavior is not something critical to the real work or the business and is something that salespeople need to attend to only when there is an HR issue (such as a personnel problem or a company crisis). As used here, understanding the narrower definition of behavior is critical to better selling and coaching as defined by the impact of what people do and the sales results they produce.

An Overview of Precision Selling Fundamentals

Precision Selling is a process for optimizing sales results by finding ways of tapping into the **discretionary effort** of salespeople. Precision Selling, which can be built into any existing sales process, shows salespeople how to add value by providing the responses that best fulfill each customer's unique needs. It identifies not just added value for the customer in the product or service but also in the relationship and interactions that occur throughout the sales process. The focus is to achieve sustainable, profitable sales through repeatable, effective activities of salespeople. Precision Selling shifts the focus from sales to the behaviors of salespeople and customers–behaviors that are leading indicators of sales results. Importantly, it is often the events that occur before, during, and after the sale that shape the choices salespeople make as they interact with their customers. The customer responses and the potential rewards and recognition the salesperson receives strongly influence the salesperson's short- and long-term behavior.

The fundamentals of Precision Selling include how to plan precise behaviors for sales activity and how to actually do those things on a consistent and constant basis. Effective planning is a necessary but not sufficient step of this work. Salespeople are paid for action and impact. Detailed planning without effective implementation, although common, is not Precision Selling. Precise planning, if not executed, amounts to a lot of extra effort without a payout. Precision Selling requires developing a viable plan and then *doing* it.

Planning. Integrating Precision Selling into the current work of the sales force requires setting up a plan. This requires linking specific behaviors to desired sales results. The following four steps are often part of effective sales preparation:

1. *Identify and define the measurable result you want.* This is the starting point of the pinpointing process, described in a later chapter.

2. *Target a customer population.* Don't target every sales call with every customer; target every sales call with X-type of customer. It is helpful to target so that you can create a challenging and attainable plan.

3. *Identify the leading indicators (customer behaviors) that serve as early signs that you* are *having an effect on the desired result.* Since you have already targeted a specific group of customers, you will only focus on that narrow

group of customers to determine fairly rapidly how or if your plan is working. If your plan is working, it will be a positive experience that you will want to repeat.

4. *Identify and define one or two critical sales behaviors.* Choose behaviors that when exhibited will produce the desired customer response (leading indicator) and the desired outcome (lagging result).

Implementing. Our plan evolves as we attempt to apply it. Precision Selling links the salesperson's words and actions (critical seller behaviors) to the desired outcome (sales results).

CRITICAL BEHAVIORS → LEADING INDICATORS → SALES RESULTS

© 2006 Aubrey Daniels International

1. Engage in the critical behaviors for each targeted customer contact.

2. Observe customer responses and, when appropriate, ask the customer if the sales call had the intended effect. Evaluate whether your sales call added value to the customer (by asking or by observing).

3. Track *what you did* and *what happened* over time.

4. Evaluate the impact of the critical seller behaviors on the leading indicators and, as time progresses, on the lagging results.

Tracking behaviors and evaluating their impact requires a certain amount of measurement and follow-up. The planning and implementing then intersect and influence each other.

Additional details are included below to provide a framework for how you might build precision into sales activities. Each of these components will be addressed in more detail in later chapters.

Precision Selling—A Coach's Perspective
What Do You Want?

The result most salespeople want is the sale—money from a paying customer. Ideally, this should be a profitable sale for the organization or perhaps optimizing the potential sale for each customer, territory, product, or service. Optimal sales results might also include identifying the best approach to each customer. An optimal result might be satisfied customers who are likely to buy later or who are likely to tell others about their experience. This approach is not just about getting more money from more customers. It is about more money from sales maintained over time on an individual case basis. For example, a salesperson may not push for a quick sale if doing so could harm a long-term sustainable relationship with the customer.

Customer targeting is an essential step in efficient selling. Potential customers who are not considered to be the kinds of customers the organization wants are a waste of the salesperson's time and the organization's resources. When left to chance, salespeople might call on the easy-to-see customers, customers who are located in convenient territories, or customers they like. Interacting with these customers may be easy, convenient, and enjoyable, but may not provide the kinds of sales results that are desired by the organization. Careful selection of customers can save time and help optimize sales efforts so that they yield the kinds of results that will pay off in the long run.

Identifying Customer Behaviors

After the desired result and the right customers have been identified, focus on the desired customer responses that your salespeople anticipate at this point in the sales cycle, early indicators that the salesperson is advancing the sale. What does the salesperson want the customer to say or do? How might the customer react? Which decision might the customer make? What might the customer say yes to now that would advance the sale? How might the salesperson use a customer's no to extend the discussion or at least get invited back?

Sales Behaviors

What does the salesperson need to do to make the right customer response happen? The salesperson might need to do effective targeting (deciding which customers to sell to), develop a useful pre-call plan, engage in one of the numerous sales call activities that make up a class of behaviors (opening, questioning, listening, sharing product knowledge, overcoming objections, presenting benefits, uncovering customer needs, closing), or complete a useful post-call analysis and documentation. The descriptions listed here are not yet specific enough behaviors in a Precision Selling sense of the word *behavior*. (For a more thorough explanation of pinpointing see chapters 7 and 9.)

How Would You Know?—Measures of Success

Once you have identified the results you want to attain, the leading indicators, and the behaviors that drive them, the next step is to identify how you might gather *evidence* of impact. We look for evidence of impact in two places: changes in the leading indicators and changes in results. Selling with precision requires gathering data to determine if the critical behaviors are occurring with enough frequency to have the desired effect. It also requires determining if the critical behaviors do in fact drive leading indicators as well as results. Determining impact can only be done reliably by using behavioral measures. Measures help salespeople and sales coaches determine *which* behaviors matter and *how* they matter. The measures provide the evidence of a relationship between behaviors and results and provide the case for monitoring both leading indicators and results.

The evidence includes traditional results measures and reporting such as market share, market share change, sales volume, and volume change. This might also include sales rankings; which, while convenient, are a barrier for producing optimal results. Rankings should not be used as a motivational device (see Daniels 1993). Rankings are usually based solely on sales results, not sales behaviors and leading indicators. Ranking based solely on sales is not typically equitable because top performers might have a rich territory or the largest account or perhaps a low sales goal from the previous year. Salespeople who demonstrate desirable behaviors as well as good results should be the ones who receive recognition.

Evidence that targeted sales behaviors are working (or not working) might also include observations of others, customer responses, self-report, and other types of behavioral data. The best measures are those that help salespeople know on their own how they are progressing from the initial customer contact to long-term, repeatable sales from that customer. Each forward movement could be used as a marker of initial success rather than waiting for the big sale to happen. The measures serve to show progress and impact, but they are also used to reinforce salespeople for doing the right things now that will pay off over time. (Further details for measuring sales results, sales behaviors, and impact are provided in chapter 10 entitled "How Would You Know?")

What Are You Going to Do About It?—Setting Expectations and Following Up

Once the results and behaviors have been pinpointed and measures have been identified, steps should be developed for putting the plan into practice and for following up. This plan shows sales coaches how to link sales behaviors, customer responses, other leading indicators, and results. This step involves more than just adequate planning; it also requires effective doing.

The sales coach may help salespeople develop plans that assist the salesperson in applying Precision Selling. They may also be of assistance in the follow-up they provide. In this final step the sales coach helps set expectations, follows up on the coaching plan to ensure that it is implemented successfully, and ensures that the plan has the desired impact on the customer and on the bottom-line results. The key here is to answer the following question: how does the sales coach provide coaching (whether it is positive or constructive) that actually *helps* the salesperson make a profitable sale?

Others within the organization (sales support, sales coaches, and sales leadership) play an important role and could either help or hinder the salesperson. The question here is this: what should sales support and leadership do to ensure that the sales coaches are supporting salespeople for engaging in optimal sales behaviors? This technique calls for a systems approach to selling and requires salespeople to consistently influence their customers and the organization within which they work. Attention from the organization often means more unproductive work and asking for permission, rather than receiving input that might actually help to advance the sale and improve customer relations. When this is the case, sometimes the salesperson just wants to be left alone. How might sales leadership and support help the salesperson and create an environment where salespeople engage in the critical behaviors (and are rewarded for those behaviors), attend to customer responses, and get good results? In this kind of environment, the top salespeople are retained and would probably recommend their organization to others. Sales coaches and salespeople have the best impact by focusing on elements that are within their realm of influence—their own behavior, the behavior of the salesperson, and the behavior of the customer. The following chapters describe how sales coaches can help salespeople best influence their customers and get the right kind of help from their organization.

Key Actions Link sales behaviors to leading indicators and sales results. Develop precise plans that ensure successful impact on your sales results rather than wishing and hoping that those results will improve. Behavioral science can provide the fundamental answer to the challenges of sales coaching.

CHAPTER THREE

PRECISION, USE, & VALUE

Speak clearly, if you speak at all; carve every word before you let it fall.

Oliver Wendell Holmes

When someone is impatient and says, "I haven't got all day," I always wonder, how can that be? How can you not have all day?

George Carlin

Symptom—Do some of your salespeople complain that their results aren't as strong as they could be because of circumstances beyond their control? Do you try to help your team, but aren't always sure how to bring about change? Do you recognize that coaching is important, but you don't have the time, and besides, you have a lot on your plate already?

Remedy—Many different coaching activities may help your team. This chapter identifies the two to three critical coaching activities that are likely to help you improve the performance of your team members and focus them on activities that are within their control.

The word *precise* in the Precision Selling context describes selling that employs specific behaviors to achieve specific results. This process removes much of the chance from selling by helping salespeople get the responses they want from customers and helping sales coaches actually help salespeople to do so. *Precision* implies several other things. It implies *exactness* and the *reduction of variance* in both the understanding of what people should do as well as the application of how they should do it. It suggests some standards and rules that guide our work practices. It implies *clarity*. It implies an *accuracy* and *correctness* based on measurement and data. Precision Selling helps to provide an exact and clearly defined description of what is happening now and what we need to do next.

I've talked with many sales professionals who have attended various sales training sessions, read a multitude of books on sales, and have heard numerous theories of selling. So why write this book since so much material already exists in this field? One reason is that sales professionals are still searching for a different kind of answer, an applicable answer, not based on motivational slogans. I've heard sales coaches say that they are looking for some help based on sound methodology. Sales coaches are looking for a way to improve their influence rather than simply making more money for the person advocating a new sales theory or method.

The focus on precision is not only about precisely describing the results that sales coaches and salespeople want to achieve. It is also about the precision of what sales coaches and salespeople *do*. It is the process of implementing effective planning that makes the difference. Granted, the act of just reading about all of this will not change your world or improve the organization's sales. Helping your sales force apply Precision Selling can change the way you manage yourself and others and it can help optimize your sales coaching skills. Sales coaches can identify and do the things that lead to their own success through the success of the sales force. It is much like managing your weight. Most people are aware that weight management is simple: exercise more and eat a balanced diet with reasonable portions. Actually doing this is a completely different matter. The failure of many diets shows us that it is not just knowledge that is important but the successful application of that knowledge.

What goals do you as a sales coach have as you read this book? To make more money? To be entertained? To learn something new? To find that you've learned enough to justify the time and money you've spent? I'd like to suggest a reason: to change at least *one* thing you do in your sales coaching that will help your salespeople sell more.

Many of the best salespeople approach their customers and their bosses in a way that resembles an experimental method: They try things and then observe what happens. If they get the desired response, they keep doing it. If they don't get the desired response, they alter their method. In a similar way, Precision Selling helps sales coaches focus on and repeat the exact activities that are proven to elicit the desired effect. While this is common sense, it is not common practice.

With Precision Selling, one first examines the baseline condition—what the seller does—and the impact of his/her action on the customer. In other words, does the customer respond with a yes or a no? Precision Selling helps you and your salespeople understand why customers behave the way they do and to influence them to do something differently if they are not yet your best fans. Even the best salespeople don't use systematic data on precise behavior. However, most successful salespeople examine their own behavior when they succeed or fail on a sales call. Unsuccessful salespeople tend to blame the customers, their boss, sales support, and others.

Salespeople can evaluate the impact they are having based on what the customer says and does. A customer saying yes, asking for something, or agreeing to a next step are all verbal signs that the sale could be moving from one stage to a more desirable stage. The customer can also signal value by providing access, granting more time, extending the sales visit, providing eye contact, or nodding in agreement. The role of the salesperson is to observe how the customer responds. What is the customer saying and doing that indicates the sales process is on track?

The best salespeople understand the importance of these observations. They don't just ask the important questions; they listen to the customer's answers. They observe the customer to see if the question they asked is really an effective question for this customer, on this day, stated in that manner, at that exact time in the conversation. They attempt to include the successful portions of their meeting in future sales plans. On the other hand, if the customer isn't responding positively, an effective salesperson attempts to alter the plan accordingly.

Prior to the call, the salesperson might even want to consider some good signs to elicit from the customer. These might be signs that they have seen before (if it is an existing customer) or signs they'd like to see in a new customer. I've heard some effective salespeople say that with new customers, any invitation to return (or more bluntly, not being thrown out) is the minimum goal.

The initial reaction to Precision Selling is that the process is just common sense and its simplicity and clarity are deceptive. One senior sales leader, Jim Burns, said, "The hardest part about all of this is its simplicity." Jim was really commenting on one portion of the process—the process of pinpointing exactly what his sales coaches needed to do to have optimal impact on his sales team and customers. Others who have used this method commented that they would have gotten there anyway and would have accomplished the end state eventually. We all know about the bravado of most salespeople, so I take it as quite an endorsement that many of them admit that Precision Selling helped them reach peak performance much faster. One sales manager went so far as to state that he would have reached his objective anyway, but by using Precision Selling, he got there in six months instead of eighteen months.

Asking a Value Question

I make it a practice to ask sales coaches specific questions about the use and value of Precision Selling. The answers to these questions help to modify the approach to make it more exact, precise, and repeatable. By asking specific questions and listening to the in-the-moment feedback, you can rapidly and continually improve sales coaching quality. For example, an unexpected benefit of initially asking questions about the method is that asking a **value question** became a permanent part of the process. Sales coaches began asking their salespeople questions that enabled better coaching. Salespeople then began to ask for more coaching since the coaching time actually became helpful.

This in turn led salespeople to begin asking their customers questions that enabled the salespeople to provide better service. Consequently those customers often became repeat customers. Salespeople would say to their customers at the end of a sales call, "We've just spent fifteen minutes talking about the value of our product and services. Tell me what was useful to you in that time. What did we talk about that will better help you with *your* customers?" By asking these quality-related questions, salespeople gathered very specific feedback from their customers about the value of the product and service as well as the value and efficacy of the sales call. This became a way to integrate reinforcement from the customer with the activities of the salesperson. This was also a way to help guide the salespeople toward repetition of their best practices and to enable them to alter practices that were not helping—not just once in a while, but every single day. They also received more informative answers from customers when they did thorough pre-call planning. The answers reinforced what they did on the call and how they prepared for the call. This was one method that helped sales coaches influence how the salespeople approached their sales.

The same method of asking a value question was used to help sales coaches as they spent time with their salespeople. Sales coaches, at the end of a joint call, field visit, or an observation with their salespeople, would say, "We've spent one hour (or one day) together. Tell me what I did today that will help you sell better tomorrow." They also asked their salespeople, "What could I have done differently on this sales visit that might have helped you sell better over the long run?" Sales coaches were often surprised to learn which of their coaching methods were or were not helpful. Sales coaches could then repeat the coaching activities that worked and alter or eliminate those that didn't work. They began to have real conversations with their salespeople about how their coaching could help their sales team sell better.

Asking a value question is really a technique for asking the customer to help salespeople connect sales behaviors to sales results and to help sales coaches connect coaching behaviors to sales results. Customers evaluate what the salesperson did on the call that will help the salesperson move the sale along, not just with this customer but with other similar customers. Also, salespeople evaluate what the sales coach does that helps them to be more successful.

This is a good time to revisit the word *behavior* in the context of Precision Selling. The word *behavior* does not imply only bad behavior as some people assume; behavior is simply *anything that a person says or does.* Behavior includes all the actions and activities of people. It is the stuff that produces reactions in others. Most sales behavior should be directed at getting certain customer responses. Most coaching behavior should be directed at helping salespeople sell better.

As mentioned previously, organizations and leaders typically view behavior to be the soft stuff, but as used here behaviors are the essential stuff—the stuff that determines the core part of any job including selling and coaching.

Precision Selling, in an attempt to connect behaviors to the desired results, relies not just on any behavior but on behavior that has impact. It is not enough that a person engages in behavior that looks good only on paper; the behavior must have the desired impact on the customer. And, in the case of sales coaches, the behavior must have the desired impact on the salesperson. The two-part process, therefore, is *behavior* and *its immediate impact on the audience of choice.*

Being precise in both your planning and your doing is good business. Precise planning requires that you specifically identify the actions that will have the desired impact. Precise doing involves ensuring that you do what you have planned, and also requires altering your actions when necessary to ensure you get the right kind of response. Precise doing also depends on plans that are workable over the long run (and that produce desirable responses). The purpose of precise planning and doing is to achieve optimal sales performance that is sustainable over the long run. The act of making precise plans and then executing them precisely is the challenge and the hard work—but the results will well reward the effort.

Key Actions Ask a **value question** at the end of your sales coaching sessions. Encourage your salespeople to ask a value question to a select group of customers who will provide useful feedback which will enable the salesperson to either continue or adjust their sales call behaviors. Sales reps will soon realize from their improved sales performance that listening to and applying valid feedback is something they do every day—not because someone told them to—but because useful things happen when they assess their impact.

CHAPTER FOUR

DISCRETIONARY EFFORT

We do not act rightly because we have virtue or excellence, but we rather have those because we have acted rightly. We are what we repeatedly do. Excellence, then, is not an act but a habit.

Aristotle

Symptom—Do your salespeople give you what you ask for—no more and no less? Are your salespeople effective at hitting their numbers but often hold back from exceeding them? How much money do you suspect your salespeople are leaving on the table?

Remedy—This chapter describes how you might evaluate the true performance potential of your team and capture some of the lost potential through precise coaching.

I've often asked sales coaches to describe their best salespeople. In particular, I ask them to describe the best salespeople who, no matter which customers they call on or the territory they are given, get the absolute most out of any situation. You can give such people any goal or any customer or any product or any weak territory, and they make the best of it.

When I ask sales coaches to identify top salespeople, that group often includes a mix of those who sell well no matter the obstacles and those who have acceptable sales numbers now (but who may not be doing the right things that will lead to sales in a lesser territory or with a lesser product). One group consists of fortunate individuals who may not focus on the right sales practices, but for some reasons beyond their control (a desirable territory, for example) find themselves with top sales numbers. Another group of individuals who may be listed as top producers are those people who for some reason are clearly focused on the right activities that drive results no matter how bleak their current prospect list or territory. The latter is the type of sales behavior that Precision Selling is most interested in replicating.

If I am talking to sales coaches and sales leaders for the first time or the thousandth time, the concept that interests them is *discretionary effort*. Discretionary effort is the key to optimal selling and is a principle derived from over seventy years of applied behavioral science research (Daniels 1989; 1993). Behavioral research helps us understand why different levels of performance occur in individuals and in organizations. We know, for instance, that performance varies within organizations and within performers over time. *Discretionary effort* describes performance over and beyond that required to keep a job or earn a paycheck. An understanding of why discretionary effort occurs or doesn't occur provides us with valuable insights into the conditions that produce minimum, average, and optimal performance.

FIGURE 1

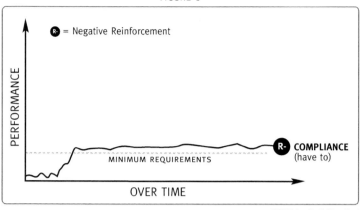

© 2006 Aubrey Daniels International

The types of performance and the time frame in which they occur are worth describing in more detail. *Performance* here is defined as getting the right results the right way. Think about the many salespeople who are out there selling to customers. There are plenty of ways to get results and to sell. Some of the sales are in the best long-term interest of the customers and the sales organizations. Some of the sales might be effective at getting dollars in the door rapidly, but are the type of sales that over the long run cannot be sustained, might not be profitable for the organization, and importantly, might eventually lead to customer dissatisfaction because the customer feels as though he or she has been taken advantage of.

Notice the compliance line in Figure 1 above. This is the level of minimal required performance—a level that individuals either discover after they complete training, figure out soon after starting the job, or determine quickly when working with a new boss. This is the line that indicates that if you perform just above it, you won't get in trouble with the boss, won't get a call from the boss, won't get fired, or will fly under the radar. It is the line that new salespeople learn about from more experienced salespeople who tell them the following:

29

- "Don't do that; you really only need to do this."

- "Forget what you learned in training; here's how you really get things done around here."

- "You're working too hard on the wrong things. Do this instead."

- "If you push too hard, they are just going to give you a higher sales objective next month/year anyway. Save some effort for later. Don't maximize your sales results right away. It will negatively affect your pay."

People quickly learn where the compliance line is; some work hard at staying just above it. They give their bosses and their organizations exactly what they asked for—no more and no less. They make enough money working half the time of others—so why exert any more effort?

These individuals tend not to be customer-focused. They may spend their time trying to avoid something that has been imposed on them by their boss or the organization. They spend time getting the administrative requirements just right. Essentially, they work hard to avoid hard work. They work less when the boss isn't looking. When the boss is visiting, they take him or her to see customers who love the product, the service, and the salesperson. These kinds of show-and-tell visits (as opposed to visits where the salesperson might actually be required to solve a business issue) are sometimes described as "milk runs."

When asked to do something by the organization, these individuals do it only when they have to. And when asked why they are doing something, whether it is following the sales process or trying something new, they say they are doing it because the boss told them to do so. Their focus is on avoiding trouble and doing the activities that people in positions of authority tell them to do, but only when they know those people are looking.

We know how these environments are created in most organizations and for most salespeople. Organizations that manage by *do-it-or-else* (also known as **negative reinforcement, R-**), tend to produce sales-people who focus on the internal requirements, even if they think the requirements are stupid or unnecessary, because their boss is making them do it. Many organizations fall into this trap and many salespeople respond accordingly. Negative reinforcement is proba-bly the most commonly used management technique. It is a method for getting behavior started by imposing a threat (a poten-tial negative consequence) that you will enact if people don't do as you tell them to do.

The reality of the compliance line is that it only works when someone is looking. The *real* performance is that they don't com-ply with the boss's requests when the boss isn't looking. The per-formance then is not always above the compliance line. Perfor-mance is only above that line when the perceived potential threat from the boss exists. When the boss isn't looking or won't find out, performance drops well below this line. When I share this informa-tion with sales coaches, they often express concern because they realize that they don't spend much time watching their salespeople. This illustrates one of the limitations of using negative reinforce-ment—the manager usually has to be there to observe in order for negative reinforcement to affect performance. Most managers can-not observe all the time, so it is possible that the performers are not doing the job as the boss expects it to be done when the boss is not watching.

Another sign of managing to the compliance line is when organ-izations continue to raise the minimum line. This approach appears to work because when the minimum compliance line is raised, eventually individuals perform to that line. Actually, this method *does* work, but not as effectively as managers and coaches surmise. Those who raise the bar often do see some sort of increase. They don't realize, however, that by managing in this manner they are forfeiting almost limitless potential, because performance is still being driven by negative reinforcement—the do-just-enough-to-get-by consequence.

The use of negative reinforcement has several residual effects. Those salespeople whom organizations want to retain often get frustrated with the constantly increasing requirements. They figure it out and resist giving too much back because they know they will only be asked for more later. They may just say, "Enough already!" and leave for an organization that doesn't raise the minimum bar every other quarter. Raising the compliance line provides a diminishing return for organizations. It may work the first few times that they do it, but they tend to get less immediate impact each time they raise the bar and ask for more. They also tend to create deep frustration and get even less performance over the long run. They may even set the compliance line so high that the possibilities are unattainable for most people in the organization. In that case, they not only frustrate but also punish the hard work of many people within the organization by holding them accountable for attaining results that are beyond their control.

There is another option—the option of creating a workplace that helps salespeople work toward optimal levels of performance. This is an environment where salespeople do a good job because they *want to* do a good job rather than because they *have to* do a good job—an environment where salespeople focus on the customer and the value they provide to the customer, and one in which salespeople don't need to be told how to do a good job. They know when they are doing a good job based on measurable and replicable customer responses. They do more than the minimum because they want to. They want to because the focus is on the impact they are having on their customers and because they have their own standards that actually exceed the organization's minimum standards. These individuals often reach out to their bosses for additional support and help because they want to operate at a high level. They are focusing on specific behaviors that add up to successful results time and time again.

Consider the profits that can be attained if each salesperson operates at his or her optimal level of performance. This kind of culture is possible when most salespeople are operating at

high-and-steady rates of performance to generate optimal revenue for themselves and the organization. The kinds of results these individuals create through their *profitable* **habits** are often sustainable because they are less interested in the quick sale and more interested in the right sale that will leave customers wanting more.

FIGURE 2

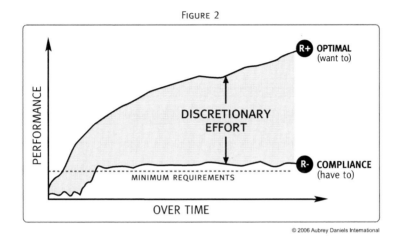

© 2006 Aubrey Daniels International

This kind of environment is created through the systematic use of **positive reinforcement (R+)** within the organization. Hold on. I sense that I might have lost you by writing that sentence. Please, give me a chance to explain. Positive reinforcement, when used systematically, can create workplaces where individuals do the right things to make good money because they want to rather than because they have to. Positive reinforcement is initially provided by leadership and sales coaches, but those sources of recognition and reward alone will not sustain this kind of environment and the profitable habits of top performers.

The creation of this type of environment begins by asking individuals to try something new or different. Even though initially they may try something new or different only because they are asked to, the coach's job is to provide plenty of positive reinforcement. This kind of reinforcement could include the usual comments about a good job, but it is also important for salespeople to have an opportunity to describe in detail the actions they took and the positive responses to their actions. A powerful reinforcer is if the new behavior works. The important issue here is that when asking others to do something new, be sure to put them in touch with the responses and reactions to the new behavior that will lead to desirable results.

All new behaviors and changes face competition from our old habits and from the extra work, time, and effort that go into trying something new. The way we are currently doing something, in many cases, probably takes us less time, work, and effort. This is even true when a new approach *might* be better, *eventually* will be better, and *probably* saves time, work, and effort. The novelty of almost any new activity poses an immediate hindrance. Therefore, we need to prepare ourselves when we attempt to do something new or different because good things don't always happen right away. Salespeople don't always get an immediate positive customer response, for instance. They will hear the word *no,* but they should be prepared to hear it and to respond to it in a way that keeps the sale going. They don't always think, Wow, this approach really *does* work better. They will probably think, this is just more work, or I could have gotten the sale anyway even without going through those extra steps.

Doing a pre-call plan, asking one extra clarifying question during a sales visit, or conducting a post-call analysis are all classic examples of activities that salespeople admit are best practices, but that many salespeople skip just because they can. They can sell without this extra effort. They can wing it. In fact, winging it might be more fun than doing those other steps. Besides, the extra effort of doing some of those other things might extend the time required to do the job and may lead to more detailed work that might not lead to more business in the call they are on right now.

Many sales programs and processes out there may seem laborious or counter to many salespeople's productivity. Precision Selling, on the other hand, starts by focusing on one small change that has the biggest impact. Fundamentally, the issue is to help salespeople examine their current selling practices and then help them identify the one area they can change that makes the greatest impact on their sales performance and results. Once this small change is made and the impact of the small change is realized, they can then identify something else to modify that will also have a noticeable, measurable impact on performance. This process includes the technique of **shaping,** which means reinforcing steady progress toward the final goal and acknowledging incremental improvements.

The question that sales coaches ask when they realize the huge potential of inspiring discretionary effort is, "How do I put people on this path to **optimal performance**?" The answer is that optimal performance can only be achieved through the systematic use of positive reinforcement and arranging the environment so that effective sales behaviors are reinforced by customers and are acknowledged to be worth the extra effort by the salespeople themselves. It also helps if salespeople become so fluent (or skilled) in the new behaviors that eventually they do not experience the new behaviors as extra work or effort.

Again, the two options for improving performance are 1) raising the bar or 2) putting someone on the path to optimal performance and shaping that performance over time. The first option elicits a limited increase, while the second accelerates positive ongoing change. Just remember that the first option—raising the bar—is accomplished through continued use of negative reinforcement, requires the constant presence or threat of an enforcer, and only brings minimal improvement.

Tapping into Your Sales Team's Potential
The discretionary effort chart, when applied to a sales team within an organization, often includes some individuals who appear at or near the compliance line, a majority somewhere in the middle, and more than a few in the upper third of the chart. Figure 3 reflects the

information regarding a typical sales team that we usually hear about from sales coaches. In many current environments, some salespeople are getting better results than others because they are already doing different things to optimize their sales. Others are doing a consistent and diligent job of hanging onto the middle ground, and others continue to hover just above the compliance line. Our analysis of this performance difference is that the organization has created this environment and that the sales leadership has allowed, even inadvertently encouraged, this kind of variance to exist within the organization. The challenge then is to influence all salespeople to optimize their sales and to help them travel the path to optimal performance.

FIGURE 3

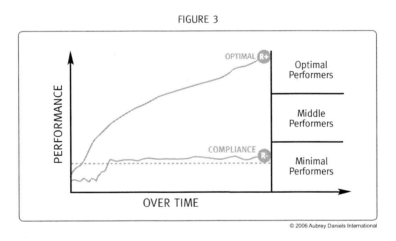

© 2006 Aubrey Daniels International

When salespeople hear that word *help,* they might get worried: "I don't want any help from my sales coach. I just want her to leave me alone." This could be a sign that the kind of help this sales coach provides is, in fact, not helpful and gets in the way of effective selling. That is possible. Many sales coaches are promoted primarily because they got high sales results, not because they showed a talent for being effective coaches. Also, they probably weren't promoted because they used effective sales behaviors; they just got good results—period. The variance within most sales teams shows the performance that is possible within any given sales organization. Some of the variance is due to having the right customers and territories, but other differences are due to the practices exhibited by the consistently high performing salespeople. This variance in performance has some good news/bad news elements. The bad news is that money is being left on the table. The good news is that the performance variance demonstrates the performance that is possible, and importantly, that by using behavioral science you can replicate this top level of performance.

Key Actions Choose to put your salespeople on the path of discretionary effort rather than just continuing to raise the bar. Creating a **want to** environment is the sales coach's only option for achieving optimal sales. Focusing on discretionary effort also helps the sales coach determine how to replicate effective sales practices that are likely to drive desirable and sustainable results.

CHAPTER FIVE

CREATING PROFITABLE HABITS

It is not the strongest of the species that survive, nor the
most intelligent, but the ones most responsive to change.

Charles Darwin

Symptom—Have you coached salespeople to help them get their heads above water, just to see them drop below the minimum level a few months later? Are you reinforced for your coaching by your sales team? Do good things happen when they take your advice? Do results improve?

Remedy—Who you coach and why you choose to coach them may have as much to do with your success as how you coach. Coaching can give you a financial return on the time and effort you put into it, especially if you find ways of focusing your sales team on the right kinds of customer responses.

Sales coaches are leaving money on the table every day, unless their team is already at optimal levels of **discretionary performance.** I have not yet met a sales coach who could not find a few minor things to change that made a big impact on sales results. In fact, the top sales coaches I've observed have quickly applied Precision Selling to help their salespeople.

FIGURE 4

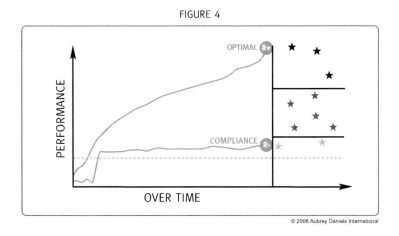

© 2006 Aubrey Daniels International

I often ask sales coaches to identify where they see their teams in terms of sales performance. I give them a blank grid (shown above) and ask them to list each salesperson by name or initials. (See Appendix 1 for samples of this grid.) Then I ask this question: if you were to spend focused time over the next six weeks to six months* actually helping one person improve the sales behaviors that impact sales results, how successful could that person get?

*(*Note: the time period is up to the sales coach, but it should be no shorter than six weeks, and typically not longer than six months.)*

Listed in the graphic on the next page is a sample description of how sales coaches might typically see the people who report to them in terms of their potential for improvement.

FIGURE 5

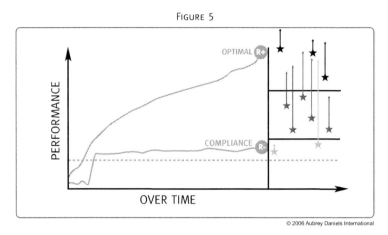

In the lower box is a person who is close to the compliance line. This person, in the coach's opinion, even with consistent support and coaching, may improve only a fraction if he received additional focused coaching support over the next six months. Sometimes a person in the lower box, with additional support once a week over the next six weeks, may move to the middle or upper box. With focused coaching, many of the people in the middle would move up within the middle box and some of them would move to the upper box. Some of the individuals would remain stable within the upper box and a few might even redefine what we thought of as optimal performance. Perhaps several of them would expand the upper limit and make even more money (in the right way) for themselves and the organization. This charting process requires the sales coaches to consider not just where people are right now, but how they might respond to additional helpful, skill-based coaching within a defined period of time. It indicates the possible performance of a sales team that has a precise focus on doing more of the right things.

I then ask the sales coaches to evaluate their coaching time and where the greatest return on investment is for them. If you improve the performance of your top salesperson versus your lowest salesperson by just 10 percent, which one will lead to more dollars sold? The answer, of course, is the top person, because 10 percent of

$100 is $10, whereas 10 percent of $1000 is $100. As an example, we worked with an organization that had about fifteen locations. We analyzed the financial gains that were possible if we chose to work with the lowest performing groups and moved them up to middle-of-the-box performance. We calculated a $15 million improvement. If we worked with the middle performing groups and helped them get within the top box, the gains would exceed $48 million. Working with the highest level would bring an even higher return. Therefore, the best return on investment comes from working with middle and high performing groups.

Of course, I don't mean to dismiss the bottom performing group. These individuals may not be performing well because they have not had useful sales coaching and would improve with focused coaching. They may not be doing well because they are in the wrong job. They may have been on performance improvement plans for so long that they are just keeping their heads above water and are glad that they're still employed. Starting your coaching work here will be very challenging. Knowing about the difficult nature of change, why would coaches try to start their own new coaching behaviors with the most challenging individuals?

The model described here intends to get coaches ready to eventually coach all individuals, even the problem performers, using a precise and repeatable process. I always recommend that sales coaches start with middle and top performers simply because those are the people who are more prone to reinforce and respond to coaching efforts. It is often punishing to work with poor performers because these individuals don't reinforce the sales coaches as much, or not at all, and perhaps will push back when coaches try to help. A beleaguered coach might then look back at his or her coaching efforts and conclude that coaching doesn't work.

The Problem Performer Dilemma

Even though I strongly recommend beginning this process with middle-level and top-level performers, coaches often ignore this advice. Individuals listening to this description of variance and potential of salespeople nod in agreement about how to best spend their time. "Yes! Work with middle- and high-level performers," they agree. Next we ask them to develop a plan to work with one of their performers, focusing on a middle- to high-level salesperson. Usually, they all agree to do just that. Then we provide our **Coaching Plan** (see Appendix 2) for them to complete.

If we don't actually walk them through the part of the plan called the **Discretionary Effort Grid,** when we collect the plans, the majority *still* target a poor performer—that one person who won't change much even if the coaches work every day over the next six months with that person. This odd phenomenon occurs consistently and we consequently spend more time than is necessary discussing this problem employee.

Why does discussion of this kind of performer consume so much time? What happens when sales coaches begin working with these performers, and what kinds of messages do they send by this coaching choice? Four issues are worth noting here.

1. *The choice of working with a problem performer says something about how some sales coaches perceive their role.* They make choices to work with their special projects because they view the primary coaching role as that of fixing problem performers.

2. *Coaches are choosing to work with someone who is unlikely to change.* If successful coaching skills are assessed by measurable improvement, these coaches are probably not being effective since they may never see any change in the performer.

3. *By focusing on a problem performer, the coach is sending the wrong message to this employee and others.* The message is probably that those being coached will perceive this additional time with the boss negatively, because it is a sign that they are not performing well. Coaching then is perceived by the rest of the sales force not as a

proactive way to develop and help but as a bailout, as punishment, or an embarrassment to the people who are selected as special projects. When coaches spend the majority of their time with problem performers, successful performers don't want the boss around.

4. *The coach also may begin to perceive the act of coaching as pure punishment.* Problem performers may push back at the coach and make the situation as unpleasant for the coach as the coach is making it for them.

This is a challenging and frustrating predicament for the salesperson and the sales coach. The salesperson is frustrated because of the extra, unwelcome attention. The sales coach is frustrated because the special projects are not changing their sales performance and they are making the coach's life more difficult each moment he spends with them. Besides, the sales coach's boss is getting on his back because he hasn't yet fixed the problem performers.

I've asked sales coaches why they tend to focus on these individuals despite the economic value of spending time with other salespeople. Here's what I've heard:

- "It is their job. Period. They shouldn't be let off the hook. I will work to the best of my ability to get them to do what they are paid to do."

- "My boss is on my back about it so I need to fix it."

- "I can't believe they aren't changing. The job wasn't that hard when I did it. I can fix this even if it takes me every waking moment."

- "They *should* be doing better."

- "I want to talk about it even if I can't change it."

- "I want to help, and it is my failure that I haven't been able to help them."

Many top sales coaches were once very effective salespeople. When they were selling, they worked with the difficult customers and figured out what was helpful and reinforcing to them. They then customized their sales approach to sell well to these initially challenging customers. When they become coaches, they sometimes lose their footing and treat all of their direct reports as if they should just follow the rules. Instead of finding out how to motivate and help their direct reports, they use a one-size-fits-all approach. The approach is often the motivators that worked for them: to be left alone, money, to have their boss just remove barriers, and so on. As many coaches eventually realize, everyone isn't the same.

Sales coaches don't always observe their direct reports' sales activity on a frequent basis. Helping direct reports do the right things when the coach is not around should be one of the coach's primary concerns. The same approach that coaches used when they sold to their challenging customers is fundamentally the same approach they need to use with their challenging direct reports: find out what is reinforcing and what will add value for them.

I often encourage sales coaches to rely on their existing HR process to solve problem performer issues, and I suggest that they not spend every waking moment dealing with these problem performers. This involves having a clear and direct conversation with problem performers, offering additional assistance to help turn around their performance, setting a time line for how long they have to turn their performance around, and then following up. This effort also includes providing clear consequences if they improve and if they don't. I advise coaches to take all of these necessary steps, and then to truly follow up with real consequences.

A word of caution is necessary here. I have worked with sales coaches who have not done the proper coaching work with underperforming salespeople. The coaches may assume that these individuals have little or no potential. Behavioral science when applied to coaching often helps coaches reexamine how they view their team members. Coaches may discover that performers they once thought of as having low potential may in fact have tremendous potential. The poor performers just haven't yet received coaching that has helped them. That said, coaches who are just beginning to learn to enhance their skills are still strongly encouraged to start not with their most challenging assignments but with individuals who, more often than not, respond positively and even enthusiastically to the coaching.

Effective salespeople know when potential customers are probably not going to buy and when to move on. They can determine, as my friend Ann Marie Rennalls says, when referencing how you might make choices if you lived in an experimental laboratory maze and learned where the dead ends are, that "there is no cheese down that tube." They determine which customers are worth their time and which ones are not. They determine which relationships are worth cultivating and which ones won't build up their book of business. But for some reason, sales coaches who were once very effective salespeople still get stuck on trying to improve poor performers.

Conversely, multiple benefits exist for working with the medium to top performers. As I mentioned, they might actually respond in a positive way to your coaching. The response might be simple like, "Thanks for working with me." The response might also include a positive change in behavior. That is, those individuals may actually take the coaching advice and try it! This might also lead to associated results improvement. Once coaches and salespeople alike see the improved results, they recognize and experience firsthand the value of the extra effort and time they have put forward. Salespeople are reinforced by trying something new and seeing how their new behaviors are paying off in the responses from their customers and from the results improvements. They might hear the word *yes* more from their customers and attribute the more desirable responses to the changes in their behavior.

Sales coaches, in turn, see the salespeople doing more of the right things and the results improve. Then the salespeople perceive the coach as helping rather than getting in the way. The salespeople may even tell their peers about this real help provided by the sales coach, and other salespeople may begin to ask for this kind of assistance: "I heard that you were working with Brian. When are you going to work with me?"

One sign of an effective coach is that individuals ask for more coaching and to spend more time with the coach. In such a case, time with the coach is not something to avoid. If employees see a coach as someone who manages by a *do-it-or-else* approach, then they try to avoid that person (to avoid the inevitable negative consequences associated with being around the coach). But if a coach actually enables individuals to try new and different things that make them more successful, that coach creates a different view of the coaching role: the role of a coach and leader who helps versus someone who micromanages and gets in the way.

Helping Those Who Help You

I encourage sales coaches to initially work with individuals who respond positively to the coaching. When they respond and begin to get good results, others will hear about it and may begin to ask you to help them too. The same holds true with salespeople who are trying something new. Ask them to try the new behavior with the customers most likely to respond positively to new sales activity. This increases the likelihood that the new behavior will work and that it will be repeated in the future.

I worked with an experienced sales coach—I'll call him Michael—who heard all this information about discretionary effort, compliance, and optimal performance. He nodded his head when I explained that working with the middle and top salespeople would give him a better return on the investment of his coaching time. He had one salesperson in the bottom third, the majority of his team of ten in the middle, and three people in the top-performer box. He indicated that he'd been a successful sales coach for years and was uncertain that he would hear anything new from me, but he also wanted an edge with his competition—not the competition in the outside world, but the competition within his organization, since sales reps and sales coaches were ranked nationally. (Read more about ranking in chapters 1 and 2.)

Michael's boss asked him and each of his peers to develop a plan for two of their salespeople. The boss discouraged them from working with their poorest performers since they'd already spent a lot of time with these people in the past and he didn't think it would help their results or their coaching effectiveness. His boss had one other caveat. He said, "Pick whoever you want as long as the two people you pick improve their placement within national rankings over the next six months. That is the outcome that I'd like to see happen."

Michael thought about it and decided the best course of action was to work with his two best reps. It seemed like a reasonable choice at first glance. However, I wanted to make sure that Michael wasn't setting himself up for trouble, since these people were already pretty high in the rankings. I asked him about it, and I was initially concerned by his answer. Michael said that both were in the first quintile nationally. When I first heard that, I asked myself, with such high ranking performers, how much room for improvement could they have? Could Michael improve their results within the six-month period? I wanted him to see the impact of his coaching and be successful with his boss. I asked him to explain his reason for selecting the top two people. His answer was informative and instructive. Here's what he said:

> I've thought about it and I think both Cathy and Jarod can improve during the next six months. They are in the top quintile, but they are just within it. I believe that not only will they improve their rankings, but if they are able to implement the plan, both could move within the top ten in the organization. There are other reasons I want to work with these individuals. Both Cathy and Jarod will teach me about the plan that we

put in place. They will apply the plan, but they will also help me modify the plan from day-one so that we are able to learn more about our customers, get better access with our customers, and extend our time with them. Ultimately, this will help Cathy and Jarod improve their overall sales. They also work well together and are located in roughly the same area. I can roll this out to both of them at the same time and follow up with them every week or two. We can meet face-to-face and continue to modify the plan. Here's another benefit: they will help make it a better plan that can be rolled out to the rest of the team. If the top two people in the division start to improve, the other salespeople in the division are going to be curious to find out how they did it. And they are going to want to get on board.

What Michael said would happen did happen. Cathy and Jarod applied the plan Michael developed to improve their overall results. Michael met with them frequently to refine the plan, and customer access, time with the customer, and the sales numbers improved. Soon, others in the sales region were more than just curious. They wanted in on the plan as well. A majority of them asked Michael to work with them: "Michael, when are you going to help us and do that thing you've done with Cathy and Jarod?"

How many sales coaches are asked by their salespeople to work with them? This is only one of the expected benefits when sales coaches help their salespeople by using effective coaching techniques. Not only that, the other salespeople who ranked in the top-third and in the middle-third got together on their own time to discuss the behaviors and results of the plan: how to do it, how to modify it to best suit their particular products and services, and how to best link it to driving better sales results. They wanted to meet with Cathy and Jarod and they also wanted to do joint sales calls with them (or have them visit with them). Michael, in the choice of working with Cathy and Jarod, set in motion the creation of a shared sales development process that the entire division embraced. Cathy and Jarod did indeed move up within the top quintile. They were both in the top five nationally that year.

This approach is relevant for sales coaches, because they can create this kind of environment for their sales team. The approach is also relevant for salespeople because it highlights actions within their control and how they might influence their own environment to put themselves and perhaps their co-workers on the path to discretionary effort. Those of us who have worked with organizations that want to optimize their sales force and tap into more of the discretionary effort of their employees are often amazed to find those few remarkable salespeople who figure out how to sell optimally even in suboptimal work environments. If others can figure it out, why not create this kind of environment for your entire sales team?

Remember that two options for elevating performance are available. One option is raising the bar (negative reinforcement with minimal returns); the other is to create an environment where the salespeople are on the path to optimal performance (positive reinforcement with maximized returns). Many organizations focus more on raising the bar of compliance rather than creating more discretionary effort. A common misperception is that creating discretionary effort is just a matter of providing more recognition, feedback, pats on the back—all that *soft* stuff. Sales coaches may perceive that all they have to do is give salespeople some nice stuff just for doing their jobs. This misperception suggests that the power of positive reinforcement is all about managers and leaders being nicer, kinder, gentler, and really working hard to be positive even when times are bad, but this approach is much more than that.

The basis of Precision Coaching is not as simplistic as it first appears. It is about managing consequences (positive and negative) to reinforce what you want and to correct what you don't want. It is also about arranging the environment (helping others tap into consequences that are available in the environment) in such a way that you put people in situations where they succeed and find reinforcers within the work (perhaps some self-reinforcers, such as "Hey, I like how that worked out" or "I did a good job there!"), as well as the right kinds of customer responses, meaning that the customer is reinforcing the right kinds of sales behaviors.

Let's look at how to help salespeople end up on the path toward optimal selling. It usually starts when a salesperson tries something new. As we now understand, this new thing that they are trying, at first, requires more work, time, and effort. Sales coaches will need to provide a great deal of positive reinforcement during this period to help the salesperson continue with the new behavior. They may try the new behavior many times before anything good happens. Initially, the new behavior is just more work with no upside. But if the sales coach is helping the salesperson stick with it, because they know that eventually good things will happen if they continue doing the new behavior, then the salesperson has a shot at achieving optimal performance.

External consequences, from the boss or perhaps a peer, are necessary to help the salesperson through this beginning stage of trying something new. The sales coach provides reinforcement for the effort even if it doesn't produce the desired customer reaction right away or each time. Eventually, if the right behavior is selected, something good will happen when the person engages in that behavior. They might say, "That worked pretty well" or "I'm comfortable doing this now" or "I'm getting better at this." They might also get different reactions from customers who support the new behavior. When salespeople persisted in trying something new I've heard customers say, "You know, many salespeople promise they are going to follow up with me, but you actually just did." Or the customer may say that the sales rep is providing some other value. The customer might even give them some new business. Even difficult customers may give access, more time, or eye contact when they didn't in the past. The customer and the salesperson (through self-recognition) eventually become stronger, more pervasive, and more consistent sources of reinforcement than the sales coach.

FIGURE 6

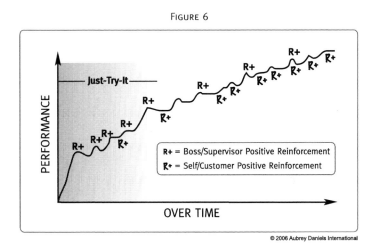

© 2006 Aubrey Daniels International

As soon as the customer reactions for the right behaviors start occurring, the sales coach can begin to fade intensive reinforcement. At this point the sales coach can be confident that the customer responses now occurring—and eventually the sales results— will provide the right kinds of support for the new behaviors of the salespeople. Over time, those on the path to optimal performance begin to experience more and more reinforcement from the work, from their customers, and from themselves. The reinforcement then begins to change the new behaviors into profitable habits. Once the behaviors become habits, they do not require more time, work, and effort. They are now fluid and easy to do. We might describe the person as **fluent** or an expert in the behaviors. Not only are the behaviors likely to pay off with better results, the new behavior becomes the preferred behavior for the salesperson. The sales coach then does not have to be as active in reinforcing the desired behaviors. Coaches can provide spot checks and support, see how they can help, and how they might keep things on track. They don't have to become so involved in the sales coaching process anymore—for that particular behavior or for that salesperson at least.

We call the time when the coach provides lots of reinforcement in the beginning and then fades the intensive reinforcement over time the **just-try-it phase.** Remember, part of this approach is for sales coaches to create reinforcing environments and to involve the salesperson and the customer as sources of change.

There are some things to be aware of when deciding how to rearrange the sales environment. Currently, many customers are reinforcing certain sales activities that may not be in the best interest of the salesperson, the sales coach, or the sales organization. Quick responses and reactive selling are common in many industries. For example, when the market fluctuates, salespeople in the financial world may get panicky calls from their clients requesting that they move money around or do something rash with the customer's investments. These types of salespeople might only talk to their customers when their customers call them. If the sales force is only responding to customer responses, they are probably not making decisions that fit their customers' overall financial plan or reaching out to their customers before risk is an issue. The salesperson who calls these customers proactively is in a better position to offer advice and to make sound decisions. The salespeople who wait for customers to call them may not have the time to sell optimally to their customers or to take actions that ultimately benefit the customer (since they are attempting to provide a quick and low-risk response).

Consider this scenario. The sales rep walks in. The customer is very busy. The salesperson respects the customer's time by making it quick and by leaving behind some samples or some materials, promising to check back at a later date. In the pharmaceutical industry, this is described as a Fed Ex or UPS sample drop. The salesperson is only dropping off samples; they are not really selling. They may be heavily reinforced for making these drops by the physician or the gatekeeper who typically prevents most salespeople from visiting with the physician. The physician may say, "Hey, thanks for making it quick; I've been really busy today." The gatekeeper might say, "Thanks for respecting the doctor's time." Yes, there are times when the salesperson needs to respect the customer's time. Yet when this occurs frequently, it becomes a performance problem for the salesperson.

Most of us have spent time in physician waiting rooms. On occasion I've seen pharmaceutical reps come and go. Some don't wait. Some just talk to the gatekeeper and leave. Others send back samples and get a physician's signature without any direct contact. Others wait and make interactions very convenient for the physician: They take out the PDA device with the signature page open. They also have their drug samples ready to go. When they meet with a physician, the physician is thrilled to make it quick and to receive some free samples. But if this were your company, would you want your sales force to spend fifteen seconds with a customer, drop off free samples that the customer can give away, and not have your salespeople even have a conversation about your product? They probably don't even have time to talk about how the drug can help patients and when it is appropriate to not give away samples (which is not profitable), but to write a prescription for the drug (which could be profitable).

In both of these examples, the customers are managing the salesperson either by reinforcing a quick, low-risk response or by reinforcing a quick, low-effort sample drop. In both cases, the salesperson may be frequently demonstrating the less desirable selling behaviors if he or she responds to the short-term customer needs. Doing these behaviors on a regular basis won't achieve optimal sales results since the activity is driven by short-term convenient customer needs (a quick visit) or salesperson needs (a short day) rather than by long-term customer needs or sales organization needs.

Rather than retraining your sale force from square-one or adding in extra steps and activities that many salespeople may interpret as extra work, start where people currently are and help them add to, alter, or fine-tune their usual selling techniques. I worked with one sales coach who persuaded her staff in this way: "Just try this new activity for a couple of months. Try it. Try something new." She specified a couple of small changes that they could make that would have a significant impact on their work. She actually made a deal with them: "Try it for two months. If it doesn't help, you can stop." This is how behavior change works. Try something new. It might be uncomfortable. It might not work every time. Try it and set *realistic* goals about what might happen.

I shared with my brother Bill and his wife Nikki (and several hundred other people) during the opening toast at their wedding reception, some free marital advice that might be useful: set low standards. Of course, my advice was intended to get a few laughs (except from my wife Mary, to whom I immediately apologized), but there is some useful advice built within this comment. I then told them that I had to amend this advice so that it was more accurate. *The real response is to have very high standards about a few things.* Determine what is important. Focus on those things, and commit to not sweat the small stuff. In other words, don't try to have it all. Focus precisely on those things in life that are essential and likely to lead to the changes you desire.

> **Key Actions** The best return on investment for your coaching time is most often found in medium- to high-performing individuals. Start your coaching efforts here to create a sales environment in which others on your team—even the poor performers—begin to ask for your help. Ask salespeople to try something new. Reinforce their efforts early and frequently. This early reinforcement bridges the gap between when they try a new behavior and when other good things happen, such as positive customer responses and sales results. The goal of the sales coach is to help put your salespeople in touch **frequently** and **consistently** with some of the good things that happen when they try something new.

CHAPTER SIX

WHY PEOPLE DO WHAT THEY DO

Logical consequences are the scarecrows of fools and the beacons of wise men.

Thomas Henry Huxley

Symptom—Have you attempted to help your salespeople by sending them to training, revising policy and procedure, or developing a new sales process, only to be frustrated that those solutions didn't work the way you thought they'd work?

Remedy—This chapter will help you analyze why your salespeople are doing what they are currently doing and what you can do about it if you want more or something different from them. Sales coaches have options beyond training. This chapter will help you focus on the likely causes of behavior so that real change can occur.

Salespeople have an almost intuitive understanding of their customers and other people. The best salespeople read their customers and they push and pull back at the right time. They overcome objections carefully. Some of the sales leaders and coaches I've worked with say they've talked to these top salespeople and asked them, "How do you do that?" Many of the top salespeople aren't talking or they are just so fluent at selling that they rarely stop to think about it.

Why *Do* People Do What They Do?

The science of human behavior has a practical answer to this question. It can help any interested sales coach understand why people do what they do, why people don't do what they are supposed to do, and what sales coaches can do about it. If they really want to influence the behavior of their salespeople or that of their salespeople's customers, then knowing this information will help them improve overall sales results.

Aubrey Daniels begins his talks at the Center for Management Research in Cambridge, Massachusetts, with a simple question for the leaders in the room, "How many of you have a problem?" Of course, almost everyone raises a hand. He continues with "How many of you would have fewer problems if others only did what they were supposed to do?" The audience nods in unison since everyone has a problem like this. The participants sit up straight at this point and begin to listen to hear the information that comes next. The cause of this important and pervasive problem is easy. Doing something to solve the problem is where the challenge lies.

One sales coach I've worked with remarked that his life would be easier if he didn't have to work with people. I'm not sure he fully realized that this really was his job since he didn't directly get his results (his salespeople did); yet he seldom interacted with his salespeople. He preferred to complain about how bad his folks were and that if he only had the right people, his results would be better. His people knew this. They might have hoped that he would eventually figure out that the best way for him to get better results was to help his team members sell better, or they might have been happy that he just left them alone and occasionally asked them to complete and send some documentation.

There is a quick answer to the questions, Why do people do what they do, and why do they not always do what they are supposed to do? The answer is because of what happens to them when they do it and what happens when they don't. Let me explain with a concrete example understood by many salespeople.

Consider the behavior of **pre-call planning.** Many sales books, models, and programs emphasize the importance of planning prior to selling. Great salespeople develop the kind of plan that is flexible and adaptable to what happens on the call. Good salespeople improve their selling when they plan their calls. What are they going to say to the customer? Which questions will they ask? What cues might they look for to determine that the customer is interested? What is a reasonable call objective? When I've talked about effective call planning in workshops, sales coaches nod their heads in agreement: yes, in general, planning helps salespeople do a better job compared to when they just wing it. Then why don't well-intentioned salespeople do a pre-plan for every call? How can we help salespeople use a pre-call plan to drive the business rather than completing the plan to comply with the boss's request? Let's apply some behavioral science to help understand the situation.

If the behavior we are interested in describing is pre-call planning we may need to further define it. Let's say we are interested in pre-call planning with a targeted group of customers. To understand why this behavior occurs or why it doesn't occur as often as we would like, it is useful to consider what happens before the behavior, what happens when we are doing the pre-call planning, and what happens after.

The events that occur prior to the behavior are called **antecedents.** An antecedent is anything that comes before or prompts the behavior of interest. Examples of antecedents are sales training, job descriptions, sales goals, your boss told you to do it, sales aids, sales tools, tip sheets, and your history. Organizations tend to do a yeoman's job of helping salespeople, coaches, and leaders get the right kinds of antecedents in place. When attempting to improve something like pre-call planning in salespeople, organizations help by providing as many antecedents as they possibly can.

- They develop training, manuals, instructions, and even motivational signs pertaining to pre-call planning.

- They create a sales aid to help people do a better job of pre-call planning.

- They remind people how important pre-call planning is to improving sales.

- They point out to their sales force that they sell better when they use pre-call planning compared to when they don't.

- They ask their salespeople to agree to do more pre-call planning.

- They remind them that it is their job to pre-call plan.

All of these examples of actions organizations typically take are antecedent solutions, which may work temporarily, but do not address the real reason why many salespeople don't pre-call plan. The key isn't in the amount of prompting for effective pre-call planning, but in what happens during or after the planning: the **consequences.**

We can identify the consequences of pre-call planning when we determine what happens when it occurs. Does it take more time to do it? Is it more work? Does it require more focused effort and thought? Might it delay the salesperson from getting to the next sales call? Might the salespeople be able to sell without planning? Might it be more fun to just wing it? The boss isn't looking anyway, so why should they plan? They can get reasonably good results anyway without doing it. These consequences are often the primary reason why most salespeople don't develop pre-call plans with targeted customers.

Consequences can be positive or negative. They occur when a behavior occurs and after. Consequences serve to strengthen or weaken future occurrences of behaviors over time. They can **include tangible consequences** like money and other stuff (such as mugs, hats, shirts, sweaters, trips, and cars). They can include **social consequences** like feedback, attention, recognition, and relationships.

Consequences can also include **natural** and **work process consequences.** When you do a certain job, certain things happen. When you hit send on an e-mail, it is sent (most of the time). Customer responses—both positive and negative—are included here as well. Customer responses in most sales jobs occur consistently and constantly during the typical day of the salesperson (in contrast to the less frequent interactions with management). All new behaviors are initially followed by negative natural consequences since they require more time, work, thought, and effort. Natural and work process consequences are so compelling because they happen immediately and so often.

One method of discovering which consequences are driving a particular performance is to review both a desired behavior and an undesired behavior using an antecedent-behavior-consequence formula called the **ABC model.** In addition, a **PIC/NIC Analysis** will be done to evaluate the relative effects of the consequences and to determine how to change them to bring about the desired changes. A desired behavior is something we want more of; an undesired behavior is one that is possibly competing with the behavior we want. In other words, the competing behavior might occur so frequently that it is getting in the way of desirable performance.

One example I've used with sales coaches is to contrast firefighting (the organizational kind, not the literal kind) with proactive coaching and developing of salespeople. In many organizations, the appeal of the emergency all-hands-on-deck approach is something many employees gravitate toward. When conducting this kind of analysis, it is first worth defining the behavior.

Firefighting can be further defined as "responding to an urgent request from your boss by the end of the day." This requires letting the boss know you are working on it and providing a solution by the time the workday ends. This also interrupts and delays planned or scheduled work.

Proactive coaching and developing can be further defined as "coaching your direct reports (exceptional, average, and poor performers) by observing their behavior and providing positive and constructive feedback at least once a day for five days."

We could pinpoint these examples even further, but for the purposes of describing the ABC model here, we can continue with the pinpoints as currently defined. The next step is to identify a list of antecedents that serve as prompts for the behavior of interest.

ANTECEDENTS	BEHAVIOR	CONSEQUENCES
A call or e-mail from your boss **A crisis exists** **History of fighting fires in the past** **Success of fighting fires in the past** **Buzz on the floor about this problem** **You've heard that top people are concerned about this issue**	Firefighting—responding to an urgent request from your boss	

ANTECEDENTS	BEHAVIOR	CONSEQUENCES
Training you've received on coaching **Boss said it was important** **It is part of your job description** **The organization has a process for doing it well** **You have a job aid to help you do this well**	Proactively coaching and developing your direct reports	

Next, let's take a look at the consequences that may occur during and after each behavior. It is important to identify the consequences from the perspective of the person doing the behavior. For the sake of these examples, think about a person who is effective at firefighting and spends a lot of time doing it. I'd also like you to think about a person who does not do much coaching and developing even though he or she states that it is an important activity for leaders to do.

ANTECEDENTS	BEHAVIOR	CONSEQUENCES
A call or e-mail from your boss	Firefighting— responding to an urgent request from your boss	**Put out fire**
A crisis exists		**Solve problem**
History of fighting fires in the past		**Avoid boss's wrath**
Success of fighting fires in the past		**Avoid complaints from senior management**
Buzz on the floor about this problem		**Avoid coaching and developing**
You've heard that top people are concerned about this issue		**Delays possibility of getting good results with the results you are accountable for**
		Could negatively impact your performance rating

ANTECEDENTS	BEHAVIOR	CONSEQUENCES
Training you've received on coaching	Proactively coaching and developing your direct reports	**Better results**
Boss said it was important		**Good performance evaluation**
It is a part of your job description		**Could earn trip to Hawaii if you get good results**
The organization has a process for doing it well		**Bonus**
You have a job aid to help you do this well		**Raise**
		Takes time
		More work
		More effort
		Conflict or disagreement with difficult employees
		Employee says thank you
		Feedback from your boss

At this point, we are ready to identify which consequences are influencing the behavior of interest. We use three dimensions to evaluate the various consequences. Some consequences are **positive** or **negative.** Some are **immediate** or **future.** Some are **certain** or **uncertain.** The most influential consequences are those that are Positive, Immediate, and Certain or those that are Negative, Immediate, and Certain. We call these **PICs** and **NICs.** PICs strengthen or maintain behavior. NICs weaken or stop behavior from occurring.

First we review and evaluate—*from the perspective of the performer*—whether the consequences of firefighting are positive (**P**) or negative (**N**).

Put out fire	**P**
Solve problem	**P**
Avoid boss's wrath	**P**
Avoid complaints from senior management	**P**
Avoid coaching and developing	**P**
Delays possibility of getting good results with the results you are accountable for	**N**
Could negatively impact your performance rating	**N**

Next, we evaluate whether the consequences for firefighting are immediate (**I**) or future (**F**).

Put out fire	**PI**
Solve problem	**PI**
Avoid boss's wrath	**PI**
Avoid complaints from senior management	**PI**
Avoid coaching and developing	**PI**
Delays possibility of getting good results with the results you are accountable for	**NF**
Could negatively impact your performance rating	**NF**

Finally, we evaluate whether the consequences for firefighting are certain (**C**) or uncertain (**U**).

Put out fire	PI**C**
Solve problem	PI**C**
Avoid boss's wrath	PI**C**
Avoid complaints from senior management	PI**C**
Avoid coaching and developing	PI**C**
Delays possibility of getting good results with the results you are accountable for	NF**U**
Could negatively impact your performance rating	NF**U**

Then we conduct a **PIC/NIC** Analysis on the desired behavior of interest to determine why it is not happening as frequently as we would like. When we conduct the analysis, we first review and evaluate *from the perspective of the performer* whether the consequences for proactive coaching and developing are positive (**P**) or negative (**N**).

Better results	**P**
Good performance evaluation	**P**
Could earn trip to Hawaii if you get good results	**P**
Bonus	**P**
Raise	**P**
Takes time	**N**
More work	**N**
More effort	**N**
Conflict or disagreement with difficult employees	**N**
Employee says thank you	**P**
Feedback from your boss	**P**

Next, we evaluate whether the consequences for proactive coaching and developing are immediate (**I**) or future (**F**):

Better results	**PF**
Good performance evaluation	**PF**
Could earn trip to Hawaii if you get good results	**PF**
Bonus	**PF**
Raise	**PF**
Takes time	**NI**
More work	**NI**
More effort	**NI**
Conflict or disagreement with difficult employees	**NI**
Employee says thank you	**PI**
Feedback from your boss	**PF**

Finally we evaluate whether the consequences for proactive coaching and developing direct reports are certain (**C**) or uncertain (**U**):

Better results	**PFU**
Good performance evaluation	**PFU**
Could earn trip to Hawaii if you get good results	**PFU**
Bonus	**PFU**
Raise	**PFU**
Takes time	**NIC**
More work	**NIC**
More effort	**NIC**
Conflict or disagreement with difficult employees*	**NIU**
Employee says thank you	**PIU**
Feedback from your boss	**PFU**

(*Note: Conflict could be certain, depending upon which person you might be providing feedback to.)

As this analysis shows, firefighting occurs for good reasons that have been supported for years within the organization. Coaching and developing, on the other hand, does not occur that frequently for equally good reasons. In this analysis, firefighting has five PICs supporting its occurrence and no NICs blocking its occurrence. The negative consequences for firefighting are future and uncertain—and are thus unlikely to interfere with that behavior.

The behavior of proactive coaching and developing, a critical management behavior, is supported by seven positive consequences, but most of the positive consequences are future and uncertain. This behavior is also influenced by at least three NICs that are pervasive challenges to increasing the frequency of coaching. In this analysis, it is unlikely that proactive coaching and developing will occur and compete with firefighting since there are no PICs supporting its occurrence and at least three NICs blocking it. Plenty of PICs support the undesired, but heavily reinforced, behavior of firefighting.

PIC/NIC Example with a Sales Behavior

Let's review a sales-related example on how to use the PIC/NIC Analysis to precisely understand a salesperson's behavior and to identify ways to change behavior. We'll return to the example of pre-call planning with targeted customers.

Step 1: Define the behavior.

Step 2: Identify potential antecedents.

ANTECEDENTS	BEHAVIOR	CONSEQUENCES
Sales training **Job expectation** **Boss asked me** **History of planning in the past** **History of getting away with not planning in the past** **Job aid** **Sales planning tool Pre-call Planning with Targeted Customers**	Pre-call planning with targeted customers	

Step 3: Identify potential consequences.

ANTECEDENTS	BEHAVIOR	CONSEQUENCES
Sales training Job expectation Boss asked me History of planning in the past History of getting away with not planning in the past Job aid Sales planning tool Pre-call Planning with Targeted Customers	Pre-call planning with targeted customers	**Good performance evaluation** **Make more money** **Make the sale** **Win that sales trip** **More work** **More effort** **Takes time** **Late for a meeting if I spend too much time on it**

Let's look at the consequences in the chart to determine which kinds of consequences these are.

Step 4: Identify whether the consequences are Positive or Negative.

In this step, we evaluate *from the perspective of the salesperson* whether the consequences listed here are either positive or negative.

Good performance evaluation	**P**
Make more money	**P**
Make the sale	**P**
Win that sales trip	**P**
Get a bigger bonus	**P**
More work	N
More effort	N
Takes time	N
Late for a meeting if I spend too much time one it	N

Step 5: Identify whether the consequences are Immediate or Future.

In this step, evaluate whether the consequences occur as the behavior is occurring, soon after, or whether the consequences occur at some point in the future. The strict definition of *immediate* is "as the behavior is occurring or immediately after it occurs." For the purposes of sales behaviors, we have extended this definition to include immediate consequences that also happen soon after the behavior of interest (within a day or so).

Good performance evaluation	**PF**
Make more money	**PF**
Make the sale	**PF**
Win that sales trip	**PF**
Get a bigger bonus	**PF**
More work	**NI**
More effort	**NI**
Takes time	**NI**
Late for a meeting if I spend too much time one it	**NI**

Step 6: Identify whether the consequences are Certain or Uncertain.

Determine if the consequences are either certain (occur every time) or uncertain (occur only some of the time or maybe not at all).

Good performance evaluation	PF**U**
Make more money	PF**U**
Make the sale	PF**U**
Win that sales trip	PF**U**
Get a bigger bonus	PF**U**
More work	NI**C**
More effort	NI**C**
Takes time	NI**C**
Late for a meeting if I spend too much time one it	NI**C**

Step 7: Examine the PICs and NICs.

In the above example, there are no PICs to support pre-call planning and there are four NICs that make it less probable that pre-call planning will occur. If you want your salespeople to do more pre-call planning, you are working against several challenging obstacles: the NICs identified here that are standing in the way of your salespeople doing pre-call plans with targeted customers. If you are a well-intentioned sales coach and you want to help your salespeople, you have plenty of competition standing in the way of helping your people prepare effective pre-call plans.

As you probably understand at this point, the mere fact that pre-call planning is a good idea (antecedent) and that it will eventually lead to more sales (a PFU consequence) isn't enough of an influence to encourage salespeople to do it on a regular basis. How many things that you want to do or that you want your salespeople to do fall into this same category? "I know it is the right thing to do or good for me but I have to wait too long for good things to happen and those good things might not even happen anyway. So just pass me the dessert!"

We'll discuss in the next chapters how to change this situation. A note of clarification might help here. We typically ask people to answer one question before we conduct a PIC/NIC Analysis: is this a *can't do* or a *won't do* issue? Put another way, could the person do what we'd like the person to do if his or her life depended on it? If the answer is no, then some sort of antecedent is required (more training, job aids, clear expectations). If the answer is yes, then the person can do the pre-call planning or the desired behavior, but for some reason (usually a sound, logical reason) the person is choosing not to do so.

Can't do problems require some form of antecedent. **Won't do problems** require understanding the consequences and changing them to help the person. This probably requires adding PICs if they don't exist or blocking NICs if they do exist. (Other possible solutions might also be required.) Antecedents help get behavior started or help to address can't do problems. They do not sustain behavior nor deal with won't do problems. They should not be used imprecisely so that someone can say, "I did my part. It is not my fault that people aren't doing what they should be doing."

Understanding and modifying consequences provides tremendous leverage to sales coaches. Top salespeople currently have many PICs that are sustaining their current level of performance. These PICs might be provided by customers or they could be provided by the salesperson. PICs might also be provided by their sales coach. How many of you reading this right now know when you do a good job? Knowing that you've done an effective job at the end of the day could serve as a powerful reinforcer (a PIC) for many salespeople. Customer and self-reinforcers are among the most powerful reinforcers available. You are always with yourself so that your own self-assessment of an effective job is an immediate consequence. The customer as a source of reinforcement is also a pervasive influence since customers influence salespeople throughout each day (and are certainly more available than the sales coach or sales leader). These customer PICs could be reinforcing the activities of short-selling, non-confrontational selling, or customer-focused selling.

Another source of PICs can be found in our work activity. Using the **Premack Principle,** when two choices exist among competing activities, first completing a less preferred activity earns the right to complete the more preferred activity. In this scenario, individuals can use their own activity and work list to organize their day and get different things done. If you have two things you must do this morning, let's say completing your expense reports and checking your e-mail, you rank the activities based on the tasks you like to do least and those you like best. (On my list, I'd put completing expense reports last.) Then you start with the least enjoyable task so that as you complete the list, the tasks become more enjoyable. An effective application of Premack would be earning the right to check your e-mail by first completing your expense reports. This does at least two things: it keeps you focused on getting your expense reports done and it gets you even more interested in checking your e-mail.

Salespeople who are having a bad day may take the afternoon off or go to the movies because there are few reinforcers available at work. This is not an example of an effective use of the Premack Principle. Instead, we are reinforcing poor performance with going to the movies. If we used Premack here to reinforce desirable sales activities, salespeople should earn the right to take the afternoon off. That would be accomplished by taking the break after you earned it—completed an important sales call, for example.

I want to go to the movies right now, but I haven't earned it yet. I will go after I revise this chapter. I would then be using one activity—going to the movies—as a reinforcer for something that isn't necessarily as fun—revising this chapter. Preferred activities can be used as PICs to arrange and reinforce some of the things you need to get done. Salespeople who are successful over time have learned to manage their reinforcers by arranging a wide range of PICs and using the Premack Principle.

NICs interfere with the good intentions of many salespeople. These NICs might be directly related to customer interactions. They include the customer saying no, conflict with customers, lack of time or access to customers, exerting effort to prepare for a customer and then having the customer back out at the last minute, and so on. These NICs might also be related to others surrounding the sale—gatekeepers who prevent the salesperson from seeing the customer and sales coaches and leaders who add extra work (such as unnecessary administrative duties) to the seller's day.

Salespeople can choose among many different behaviors when dealing with customers or when managing their own activities. Some of the choices take more time, work, and effort (all NICs). These choices have little chance of occurring at a high rate. Other choices take less time, less work, and less effort (all PICs). All things being equal, people go for PICs unless those things that take more time, work, and effort are reinforced in other ways. These are often the choices salespeople make, even if a good plan (or any other best practice that may be a NIC) might help them sell better. The challenge then for sale coaches is to help structure every salesperson's day so that good things (PICs) support the best practices. When this occurs, the desired behaviors are not inherently linked to NICs. Fluent behaviors or profitable habits are supported by PICs.

In the next chapter we will begin to discuss how to develop a sales coaching plan that supports desirable behaviors that lead to increased sales. This process links sales behaviors to measurable results. The plan includes reinforcers from the customer, the salesperson, and the coach. The plan also includes a process to help sales coaches be clear and precise about the behaviors and results they want as well as how to evaluate the effectiveness of their coaching.

Key Action Invest your coaching time in the consequences that influence desired behavior change. Provide PICs for new behaviors you identify that lead to desirable, long-term sales. Manage the antecedents and consequences that create optimal sales environments for salespeople.

CHAPTER SEVEN

PINPOINTING

Everything is vague to a degree you do not realize till you have tried to make it precise.

Bertrand Russell

Symptom—Have you ever said, "I know what it will look like when I see it" or "That's not what I meant?" The general requests that you make to your salespeople may leave a lot to interpretation. Pinpointing takes out much of the chance and guesswork so that effective selling can occur.

Remedy—This chapter provides tips and suggestions to help you convert your ideas and thoughts into specific and objective descriptions so that your salespeople know what to do.

Pinpointing is the important work of being very specific about the behaviors that drive the desired results. Let's consider the above quote by Bertrand Russell. Pinpointing is the work of clarifying what you mean in terms of your own behavior and the behavior of others. Pinpointing helps salespeople be clear about exactly what they need to do to attain desired results. Pinpointing helps sales coaches clearly state their expectations.

I've heard sales coaches talk about asking people to do something basic like *interviewing customers* during a sales call. They have been frustrated that few people are getting what interviewing means so they send them to training two, three, or maybe four times. Using an ABC model, we determine that the problem usually isn't that people don't know how to interview. Most people are not interviewing because of what happens during and after they do it—a consequence issue. Interviewing takes more time, extra effort, and sometimes customers ask the salespeople additional questions for which they may not have adequate answers. They may also lose control of the call when they stop talking and when the customer answers the questions. To top it all off, their bosses yell at them when their call times are higher than average or when they don't make enough calls in a given day. It seems that interviewing just doesn't pay in the moment.

Although salespeople often don't interview because of the associated consequences, part of the issue is an antecedent issue: the exact behavior of interviewing is not precisely defined. The vague word *interviewing* is left to interpretation. Skilled salespeople do it well. They also impact their customers in a positive way. When you ask them what they do when they interview, they are clear about the words they use and the questions they ask. Interviewing is not something they do because their boss asked them to do it. They do it because it makes sense and elicits the right customer reaction.

Here is a drill-down from the vague word *interviewing* to a more precise description of how people might approach interviewing.

Interviewing

1. Ask customers a question.

2. Ask customers an open-ended question.

3. Ask customers an open-ended question about their business.

4. Ask customers an open-ended question about their business to identify customer needs.

5. Ask customers an open-ended question about their business to prompt them to talk about how they might use their phones to conduct business.

6. Ask customers an open-ended question about their business to prompt conversation about how they might use their phones to conduct business. Before contacting new customers, make a list of possible customer responses, effective follow-up questions, and answers to their responses.

We could continue to pinpoint the process of interviewing even further. We pinpoint with enough specificity so that the salesperson understands exactly what the sales coach expects and so that the salesperson's actions have the desired impact on the customer. If all a coach says is "Go out and sell" and then the salespeople go out and interview in the way described (in number six above), then the coach may not need to do the work of pinpointing. But how often is that the case?

As you begin to define what you want salespeople to do you may wonder, how much pinpointing is necessary? A pinpoint must provide enough clear information to tell the salesperson how to do the right work and do it well. Pinpointing helps to reduce the variability that occurs when we use vague words such as *interviewing, closing,* and *selling.*

Let's use a process to help us pinpoint what we expect from ourselves and others. First we will focus on identifying all the important specifics that we know. Then we revise these specifics to ensure that the specifics are observable, measurable, and reliable. These dimensions provide help to pinpoint the behaviors and results you want so that it is easier to measure, reinforce, and change performance. Applying these dimensions to your pinpoints improves the objectivity of observations and allows clear communication of your expectations. Pinpointing helps sales coaches develop clear expectations, put those expectations into practice, and evaluate their impact.

Specific. Start the process of pinpointing by identifying details which include answers to *who, what, how, when, where:* clarify what you want someone to do. For instance, take *sharing key product information with a customer* as a potential behavior. The pinpoint would be more precise if we identified other details such as *with whom* they might share this information. Does this mean that we share product information with all customers? Should we share with a targeted list of customers? Which customers would benefit most from this shared information? This pinpoint could also include more details on the *what.* Does sharing mean just reading the sales presentation? Is it just pointing to the sales brochure? *How* the salesperson shares information is also important. I've known many salespeople who just want to read the sales presentation. If they are stopped in the middle, they might even lose their place. The *how* might include stopping and pausing occasionally to get the customer response to see if they are receiving the information the way you are intending to send it. As the Celtic great, Red Auerbach, said as he described his coaching, "It's not what you say; it's what they hear." The *when* and *where* may be important to specificity as well. *When* you ask a question may be more important than *if* you ask the question, especially if asking it at the wrong time confuses customers or encourages them to say no before they are aware of how the product or service can help them.

You might have noticed that the word *why* was not included in this discussion. The why is not part of an objective description. In fact, try to stay clear of the why. Why did the customer do or not do that? Was it because they don't like our product, or they don't want to hear it? Why did salespeople do or not do that? Were they just lazy or undisciplined, or don't they really believe in this product? Why did the sales coach do or not do that? Is it because the sales coach is really just checking things off the box and is only spending time with salespeople because the boss is asking him or her to do so? When pinpointing, the answers to the why question shift our focus from the knowable and observable to opinions and interpretations about what might be. By shifting to the why, we shift the discussion away from what we want salespeople to *do*. We tend to shift it to something less useful—to whether or not our interpretations and guesses were on target. The why opens up debate and disagreement over what was or was not seen rather than how we might coach better. An argument over why we think a salesperson did something rarely helps us coach better and often makes future coaching less effective. If you really must discuss why, just ask the salesperson or the customers point blank. Remember that assuming the why usually shifts the focus from your intent to provide help and feedback to a challenge of your interpretation.

Observable. This is the step in the pinpointing process in which we refine our pinpoints by ensuring that we are focusing on observable behavior. A pinpointed behavior is something that someone is doing that we can see or hear, such as the words that people say or the expressions that they make. A pinpointed result is observable.

Observable pinpoints help us steer clear of assumptions, perceived attitudes, feelings, inclinations, and interpretations of what we think is going on inside someone's head. Labels and generalities are inferences that go beyond direct observations and often hinder our ability to develop clear and objective pinpoints.

The behavior of observing customers as well as salespeople is critical to coaching effectiveness. Observing is a key leadership, coaching, and sales skill. As Komaki (1998) describes in her book, *Leadership from an Operant Perspective,* "The research demonstrates that leaders who monitor [i.e., directly observe] and provide consequences will have followers who perform better and have more positive attitudes about their leaders" (p. 130). This finding is also highly relevant to the act of selling; successful sellers are effective observers of customer behaviors. Consider the best salespeople with whom you work. Can you recall how they talk about customers' words and actions? I suspect they focus on customer behaviors consistently and constantly.

Measurable. Is the behavior or result you want to observe measurable? Have you stated the pinpoint in terms of how often, how many, how frequently? Have you indicated any qualitative descriptions of the behavior (how well)? How would you know if the salesperson had done the behavior correctly? Be clear about the measures when identifying what you want from a direct report. One pharmaceutical salesperson I worked with visited several clients over a six-month period. During each sales visit, one physician (a customer) committed to writing prescriptions of a certain drug based on patient needs. When the salesperson examined sales reports showing the exact product amount being sold, she observed that this physician (who had promised so much over the time period) actually only wrote a small number of prescriptions for her product. When applied to sales in general, the issue here is that the customer said he was buying, but the actual numbers didn't match his promises. On the next visit, the sales rep asked the physician to actually write more prescriptions. (For non-pharmaceutical salespeople this would be equivalent to buying the product.) She pointed out that the doctor was only writing about two prescriptions per month. (She was expecting over 20 per month.) She asked the physician to talk with her about this discrepancy so she could understand why he wasn't writing more prescriptions. After discussing this situation with her sales coach and a few clarifications about the product with her customer, the customer actually started to prescribe more of that drug. She reinforced the customer for sharing his concerns and for taking the time to talk about the situation in a way that would eventually lead to an actual increase in her sales.

Reliable. Reliable refers to whether two or more reasonable people would have the same count of a pinpointed behavior. The agreement among observers is the important focus here. If we are talking about observing customer behavior, a pinpoint would be one that when two or more salespeople say that the customer offered a commitment (said yes to something), we could agree that they offered a commitment about the same thing.

Another part of this is whether the customer, in fact, would agree with the salesperson's observation. Salespeople seldom ask customers outright if their understanding of the customer's needs and requests are reliable, but disciplined salespeople will recap the specifics that the customer agreed upon in an attempt to remove doubt and gain consensus.

Mark Repkin, of Certif-A-Gift in Chicago, is a consummate salesperson and sales leader, and one of the best I've seen at ensuring that he and his customers have come to a common understanding. He does so by verbally summarizing what he and the customer have committed to during the sales call. If anything, all those who are part of a sales call with Mark (all the sellers and all the customers) are clear about what happened and what the next steps are. Mark doesn't just assume reliability (what people may be thinking). He asks for it to be stated out loud during the sales call. He brings that same kind of skill when he is offering sales coaching to his sales team: clarity from his salespeople about what he expects, how they might improve their sales, and how Mark might help them.

Reliability is an important part of the feedback discussions that sales coaches and leaders should have with their direct reports. It's easy for a group of sales coaches to make poorly pinpointed observations about the salesperson's skills after watching a video:

- This salesperson was not customer focused.

- This salesperson did not close effectively.

- This salesperson did not overcome objections sufficiently.

All the sales coaches nod in agreement, which in this case means that *they* have met the pinpoint criterion for reliability. When asked the question, would the salesperson you observed on a sales call see it the way you are seeing it? most sales coaches concede that this is the challenge. The missing behaviors are clear to them, but may not be so clear to the person they are trying to help. Gaining agreement with the person receiving the feedback is a necessary condition if that feedback is to have the intended impact.

Sometimes when helping sales coaches pinpoint what they want their salespeople to do, we discover that the initial behavior of interest isn't really the issue. A classic example is **closing.** The film *Glengarry Glen Ross* (1992), based on David Mamet's play of the same name, highlights the need for salespeople to close when they talk about another version of the ABCs—"Always Be Closing." The sales manager in the film assumes that sales increase if salespeople close more often. *Closing* can be interpreted in a variety of ways. Fundamentally, it is defined as "the behavior of prompting the customer to commit to buying something from the salesperson, or if that is not possible, to commit to some next step with the salesperson." How to make this happen can vary. Closing is not just aggressively asking for the business as in the *Glengarry Glen Ross* version. Closing usually includes other behaviors. The success of an effective closer often lies in what happens prior to asking directly for the business.

Sales coaches frequently express frustration with salespeople who struggle with closing. For example, I was riding along with a pharmaceutical industry salesperson (Ken) and an exceptionally skilled sales coach (Elissa). The salespeople in this industry call on their top sales targets, who are typically physicians, every week or at least once a month. They don't have to get all the business during one customer visit. They are not selling directly to their customers, but they are influencing physicians to write prescriptions for their product. Because of this set-up, effective selling often occurs over the course of many different visits.

During this particular call, Elissa told me that she'd been working with Ken on his closing skills. Ken was known for being very strong in the area of customer service, but he reported feeling uncomfortable with closing. So we went on a few calls. In the car, Ken described his plan for the day and indicated that he really needed help in closing. He described the steps in the sales process, defined closing, and provided several examples of closing. Ken and Elissa even did a role play on closing prior to one of the sales visits.

We observed Ken on about six calls that day, and each time he attempted to close. I'm certain he wanted to make a good impression and he succeeded because he closed on all six calls. There was some variance, however, on each call regarding when he closed, how he closed, and how successful his closes were. These closing variances and the events that followed the closings provided clues for us as we attempted to help Ken.

Let's take two extreme examples from the closings that day. In one example, Ken provided some information to a physician and asked some of the right questions to identify the concerns of the physician's patients. He engaged the physician in a discussion that lasted about ten minutes longer than he had spent in most typical encounters, and he was clearly providing value during this time. Throughout the conversation, Ken asked specific questions and the physician usually answered yes. At the end of the sales call, Ken very naturally and fluently started and completed his close. He got a great response from the physician who seemed thankful for Ken's time and offered a commitment to Ken.

Right after this fluid, effective call, Ken had another call. This physician was considered difficult to pin down and a sales rep was lucky to have more than five minutes of his time. The office was very busy but Ken began the call and provided the physician with information about the product. He did manage to receive one yes answer to one of his questions (a preliminary or trial-type close). When Ken shifted to start closing for the doctor's commitment, I could see the gap in the presentation and I could see Ken struggling to jump this Grand Canyon of a gap by awkwardly shifting to his close. In my mind, I was shouting, No! Not yet! If you ask for the business now, you will show the customer that you haven't been listening to what he has been saying. There isn't sufficient groundwork to justify closing at this point!

Okay, I might have just thought, No! No! Don't go there yet! Nevertheless, since neither of us was telepathic, Ken started and completed his close. I think the physician glared at Elissa and me at this point—sort of indicating that Ken wouldn't have done that if we weren't there. Then the physician said something like, "Well, no, I'm not ready to do that yet. Haven't you been listening to what I've been saying?"

At the end of the day, we discussed Ken's selling skills and his strong desire to be a better closer. When asked to describe how he thought the day went, he indicated that he had closed on all six calls, but that some were better closes than others. We asked him to describe his best and worst close of the day. He picked the two examples described here. We asked him to describe each call. At first, Ken did not recognize the differences in the calls that we observed. On both calls, Ken followed the same closing script. He used almost the same words and asked the customers for their commitments in the same way. We asked him to describe the differences in the calls *before* he started his closing. Here is where Ken began to clearly understand and describe the differences. On the first call, Ken indicated that he *earned the right to close* based on the customer's responses. On the second call, he now understood that he had not earned the right to close. He thought that he closed at the wrong time, and that he didn't do some things on the call that would have made it reasonable for him to close when he did. He also indicated that he probably would not have closed had we not been there, because he didn't feel the timing was right with that challenging customer. He had not matched his words and actions to where the customer was in the sales cycle.

The point here is that certain performance problems are not

always what you think they are. Here the problem actually was one of closing too fast, not the actual closing. A performance problem often occurs when we least expect it—in this case during the sales process, not at the end of the process. Organizations have used improved closing as a potential quick fix to improve their results. Individuals can increase the frequency of closing, but this quick solution does not always lead to sustainable behavior change and sustainable impact on the bottom-line results. The focus shouldn't be exclusively on closing; it should be on when to close, how to close, and with whom to close. Further pinpointing of a perceived solution can always improve your chances of getting the behaviors and results that you intend to get.

Effective behavioral pinpoints also include the following dimensions.

Linkage. Effective pinpoints are linked to critical leading indicators and results that are important to the performer or the organization. I've seen pinpoints over the years that are incredibly clear and objective but that doubtfully drive business results. I've seen great plans on helping people call on more customers. However, focusing only on the number of sales calls might leave your sales team with more calls and more work but not more sales. Focusing on a professional look or an exact scripted presentation may get you good appearances and impressions, but the change might not drive sales. I've also seen coaches in customer service organizations focus on elements like the right greeting and opening or a professional tone and manner. These may be reasonable pinpoints, but they usually don't drive critical results for the organization. Salespeople may improve their tone, manner, appearance, greetings, and openings, but if this is where the plan stops, all the company has gained is some well-mannered salespeople who may not sell that much and who may not provide enough *value* to the customers to ever get their business.

Controllable. It is quite a challenge to sell if you don't have a successful product, if the economy is tanking, or other factors are beyond your control, especially if your boss is asking for more. Under some conditions, *more* may not be within your control: Less erosion of your market share might be. Being on top within a down market might be. There might be other goals that are more within one's control during times of economic strife, for example, goals that can keep one on track. The best goals are challenging (meaning better than you are doing now) and attainable. An unattainable goal could push salespeople to take shortcuts that are not in their best interest or in the best interest of the organization. I caution sales leaders who might be tempted to demand growth at all costs during challenging times. You might get growth, but you might also have a mess on your hands after your sales force takes some shortcuts that help them adapt to your requirements. If you want to push growth, be sure to be clear about the legitimate ways to achieve it.

Active. An active pinpoint describes something we want rather than something we don't want. If the pinpoint starts with the words *don't* or *stop,* it is a sign that the pinpoint is not active. Let's consider an example to help describe active pinpoints and to illustrate why stating them in an active way actually helps you get what you want.

I worked with Jack, a sales leader who was struggling with managing a large number of sales coaches and sales reps who sold telephone business services. They all worked in a large call center with plenty of distractions and a large amount of responsibility for the sales coaches. Some of them managed up to twenty-five salespeople. Historically, these sales coaches received good pay and bonuses if the center met its goals and if they met their team-level goals. The savvy sales coaches worked hard at getting the right salespeople on their teams and then spent the rest of the time doing other things.

At one point, Jack got frustrated with his sales coaching team because they were not coaching and developing their direct reports on a frequent basis. He asked them to increase the frequency and they all agreed that it was the most important thing that they should be doing. They estimated that they should be spending about 80 percent of their time coaching their staff members. They were currently coaching their people about 15 percent of the time. After they stated that it was the most important part of their job, Jack expected to find that coaching would increase. It didn't. So he asked them again. They promised again, but coaching time didn't go up much beyond 15 percent.

We then started to examine the consequences for coaching and developing. We found that a few of the coaches supported their salespeople adequately, but plenty of other reinforcers supported alternative behaviors such as attending meetings, doing administrative work, being on conference calls, taking over sales contacts, being on special projects, and listening to concerns from employees. Jack got people to stop attending duplicate meetings and being on special projects—this was within his control. He then attempted to free up more of the sales coaches' time by helping them to eliminate or delegate some administrative work.

Each of the sales coaches on Jack's team was responsible for several reports (some were sales reports, others were service reports, while still others were productivity reports...yes, they had lots of reports). These reports grew in number over the years and the organization relied on components of many of them. Jack expected that by eliminating the reports (which probably consumed about a day or a day and half per week per coach) the coaches would begin coaching and developing more frequently. He therefore issued the order that they stop doing administrative work. Each week thereafter his team members reported that they weren't spending their time working on administrative reports. Still, Jack did not see an increase in coaching and developing. And he did not see the decrease in administrative work. What he did find out was that virtually all of the coaches were still somehow doing the administrative work. Some of them were taking the work home and doing it during the evening. Others were doing the administrative work during their lunch hours, while still others did it over the weekend.

Some just blatantly did it during the workday. One person came into work by six a.m. so that Jack wouldn't catch her working on the reports.

Two problems existed here. The first problem was that few reinforcers were in place for coaching and developing. Jack hadn't provided any. He also didn't arrange the work environment so that there were more reinforcers for coaching and developing than there were for other activities. The second problem was that Jack didn't state clearly the behaviors that he wanted his staff to do. He set himself up to *catch them* doing administrative work but he did not prepare himself to reinforce them for doing something different. You can only truly reinforce the behavior of interest when the desired behavior is stated in an active way. When they appeared to be doing nothing, they were not doing administrative work. As you read this, I'd like to thank you for not doing administrative work. "Not doing administrative work" is something anyone can *not* do...even a dead person does not do administrative work. In this case, Jack could reinforce his team for doing nothing. But that wouldn't reinforce the activity that he really wanted. Jack needed to define the pinpoint in an active way.

Jack finally identified an active pinpoint for his team: to transition one piece of administrative work each week to a person they could identify and train. He also asked them to check the quality of the work to ensure it was done correctly. Jack asked them each week to tell him which report they would transition and to whom they might transition it. He then asked for their plans for getting the people they trained up to speed on doing the reports well and for their plan for checking to ensure quality completion of the reports.

This did require some precise, additional work and effort, but it was much less work than the game they had been playing with Jack. It was also less work for the sales coaches who for years (perhaps over a fifty-year period in the organization and twenty-five years for some of the sales coaches who worked there) had done their jobs the traditional way. After all, the sales coaches had been reinforced for years for doing administrative work, so their old habits were not going to change overnight. Such habits certainly weren't going to change just because Jack asked (and then told) them to change (both weak antecedents).

Performance started to change only when he told them what he wanted: transition the work to someone else and be accountable for checking that the reports are done correctly. He could then provide positive reinforcement for the coaches' efforts. Within six weeks, their behavior—behavior that had been reinforced for decades—changed for the better. The active statement of what Jack wanted helped them see what they were *to do* rather than what they were *to try not to do*. The active statement of the behavior also helped Jack reinforce them on at least a weekly basis. He could ask them each week about how they were transitioning pieces of their work. Previous to stating what he wanted his staff to do in active terms, all that Jack was prepared to do was catch them doing something wrong and then getting angry with them when he caught them. The active pinpoint focused Jack on behavior that he could positively reinforce.

Pinpointing provides clarity for sellers, their customers, and sales coaches who are attempting to help sellers have a better impact on their customers. This clarity helps to identify the exact behavior needed to have the desired impact. This exactness not only saves time, it helps guide successful selling so that critical behaviors are done and done in a way that has the desired impact on others. In the next chapters, we will review how to gain business impact through the process of pinpointing and learn how behavior analysis can be used to best influence your own behavior as well as the behavior of others.

Key Actions Take the time to clarify the behaviors and results that you want by describing them in a way that is specific, observable, measurable, and reliable. Ensure that what you ask people to do is linked to an important result and the organization's strategy, is within the control of the performer, and is stated in an active way.

CHAPTER EIGHT

QUICK & PRECISE PLANNING

He who is prepared has his battle half fought.

Cervantes

Symptom—Planning is typically just more work and it often really doesn't get me what I want in the end. I know planning should help, but how can I get people to really plan, not just to comply with my request but to really drive business with their customers?

Remedy—Learn to develop plans that have impact and drive the business. Be sure to build in reinforcers for you, your salespeople, and customers so that your plans work and are sustainable.

Sales coaches may have heard some of the following comments from their salespeople: "I'd plan if I weren't so busy." "I don't have time to plan." "Planners plan; sellers sell." "Good salespeople don't need to plan." "The best salespeople know when to drop the plan and sell." Some of these remarks may be valid, because many of the best salespeople can get by without planning or perhaps the planning they've done in the past has not been that helpful. This chapter describes a quick, precise way to help salespeople plan. This planning will, in turn, help coaches coach more effectively. I have emphasized the word *quick,* because in some cases the planning for an individual call may take less than five minutes if the right work has been completed beforehand and when the right post-call analysis is done after the previous sales call. The word *precise* is also worth clarifying since the coaching process described here involves doing a few critical things that lead to success.

Steps for Quick and Precise Coaching

1. Develop a plan that identifies the results you want, the customer responses you want the salesperson to elicit, and the actions that you want the salesperson to take.

2. Identify how the results, the customer responses, and the seller behaviors will be measured so that progress can be tracked and reinforcement can be provided.

3. Identify the activities that you as a sales coach are willing to do on a daily, weekly, and monthly basis that will ensure that you will get what you want. Also make sure that you build reinforcers into your plan to sustain it.

The goal here is to help coaches achieve optimal selling by pinpointing behaviors and results and building in the antecedents and consequences that attain the desired goals. The plan is precise because the model can guide you to select those antecedents that are critical to your success (such as clarifying your expectations and ensuring that salespeople have the proper tools and training). This part of the plan takes care of any can't do issues. Once this part of the plan is complete, and once sales behaviors and results are adequately pinpointed, consequences can be modified to help achieve optimal sales results through focused coaching.

COACHING PLAN

What Do You Want?

PINPOINT

Result:

Leading Indicator: Desired customer response

Behavior: What is the salesperson going to do?

How Would You Know?

MEASURE

Result:

Leading Indicator: Desired customer response

Behavior: What is the salesperson going to do?

What Are You Going To Do About It?

FOLLOW UP

© 2006 Aubrey Daniels International

Behavioral science focuses on two elements: using proven methods to pinpoint and link behaviors to results and an evaluation of how the consequences (and to a lesser extent the antecedents) are influencing customer, salesperson, and sales coaching behaviors. We've spent some time in previous chapters discussing the subjects of pinpointing, leading indicators, and results, as well as linking the right behaviors to the right results. In this section, we are going to examine the types of consequences that impact coaches, customers, and sellers. Further descriptions of the different types of consequences are found in Daniels (1989; 1993; 2003) and the writings of other prominent, pragmatic behaviorists (Skinner 1953).

We will examine principally five kinds of consequences here: positive reinforcement, negative reinforcement, punishment, penalty, and extinction.

Consequences are evaluated in terms of the effects that they have (and are not necessarily negative as is often implied in the everyday use of the term *consequences*). If your intentions are to increase the likelihood that a behavior will occur again, your choice is to use either positive reinforcement or negative reinforcement.

A **positive reinforcer** is any consequence that follows a behavior that increases the occurrence of the behavior in the future. Examples of potential positive reinforcers are positive feedback, access to preferred work, money, winning, and earning trips. The problem with listing the kinds of objects or activities that could be positively reinforcing is that the objects or activities, in and of themselves, are not important. The important question is does the consequence increase or decrease the future occurrence of the behavior? A consequence is only positively reinforcing when it increases the behavior in the future.

Negative reinforcement also increases behavior but has a different kind of impact. Negative reinforcement is the do-this-or-else approach to increasing behavior and it creates escape-or-avoidance behavior. In other words, the performer increases some behavior to avoid getting in trouble, getting fired, getting more unwanted work from someone, or receiving other forms of negative attention.

Deadlines are, more often than not, negative reinforcers. I may work not to miss my deadline, but I may not work smarter or ahead of time to complete the work before my deadline. If negative reinforcement is used sparingly, it can be a useful tool for managers and coaches. When there is no behavior to positively reinforce, negative reinforcement may be used to get the salesperson's attention and to get the behavior started. Negative reinforcement will not lead to optimal performance, however, and is not effective when you want someone to do something when no one is looking. Your goal is for performers to do something because they want to. Negative reinforcement also has some side effects such as low morale and resentment that make its overuse undesirable.

Two primary consequences work to lessen, weaken, or stop behavior from occurring: punishment and penalty. Both punishment and penalty stop or decrease the future occurrence of a behavior. **Punishment,** loosely defined, is getting something you don't want whereas **penalty** is losing something you already have. In both cases, the future occurrence of the behavior is either weakened or eliminated.

Extinction, defined here as the removal of reinforcement, provides a further understanding of why certain types of behavior occur or don't occur. Extinction occurs when a previously reinforced behavior fails to produce a reinforcer. With extinction, the frequency of the behavior gradually decreases, and then disappears over time. Extinction is most commonly associated with such concepts as burnout, low performers, and poor paperwork habits.

A common example of how extinction might be effectively used in organizations is in the management of complaining. When people complain, they are probably being reinforced for it, because when they complain, people listen. Others might also commiserate with the person who is complaining: "I agree. Can you believe what they did this time?"

When individuals complain, they often get an audience. People listen and say how bad they feel for this individual. Complainers might also hear acknowledgment from others about how hard they work. They get extra or special treatment from someone (peers, their boss, others) who provide an audience for the complaining. In some organizations, complaining has been reinforced so often that it is a characteristic of the workplace. Therefore, complaining occurs very frequently, so much so that those activities interfere with work. This situation usually occurs because the behaviors are being reinforced by someone within the organization. Extinction is an excellent option for helping to minimize certain annoying behaviors such as complaining. Extinction involves the slow and gradual decline of a behavior when the expected reinforcers (listening, commiserating) are withheld.

Extinction is more useful than punishment or penalty for nuisance behaviors. When used to solve annoying behaviors like complaining, using punishment may actually affect not only the behavior that you desire to change (the complaining) but other important and desired behaviors as well, such as people talking to their managers about relevant issues, people sharing legitimate concerns with their coaches and managers, or discussing situations before they get out of control.

Which consequences are important to sales? The quick answer is all of them, including extinction, depending upon what a sales coach wants to accomplish. Figuring out which consequences are operating for your salespeople, with their customers, or with a sales coach is critical to effective and efficient coaching.

What do customers want? This question might be rephrased to be more precise: what do customers find reinforcing? Once this question is answered, coaches are on their way to not only helping salespeople sell to customers once, but to attain repeat, long-term customers. The next question after we consider what might be reinforcing to customers is, which reinforcers are positive, immediate, and certain (PICs) for customers? Keep in mind that reinforcement is very personal, so it is critical to identify the unique reinforcers of every customer.

Customers differ in significant ways. Some customers want

information; others want social contact. Some want style; others want substance. One customer wants salespeople to make it quick, while another customer wants to spar or even to disagree with salespeople for a while before they give in to the sale. In each case, it's important to identify the products or services that customers need (usually a reinforcer) as well as *how* they prefer to reach the point of final sale. In other words, appreciating the destination really may be determined for some customers by how much they enjoy the journey.

B. F. Skinner (1953) remarked that the "subject matter, not the scientist, knows best" (p. 13). He was describing how his view of behavioral science worked: One can attempt to determine the intended causes and effects, but in the end, the only way we know if a consequence is reinforcing or punishing is by observing the behavior of individuals after they have experienced that consequence. If the behavior of the subject (the customer, the salesperson, the sales coach, the boss) increases, some form of reinforcement is at work. If the behavior decreases, punishment, penalty, or extinction is operating. By looking at changes in behavior, the coach can quickly identify which consequences are at work and also know which consequences will modify behavior in the desired direction.

Many behavioral scientists misunderstand Skinner's point as they look for singular causes that have a direct link to their effects. They are looking for simple inputs (causes) and outputs (effects). Skinner's approach doesn't quite work this way. Instead, during most human interactions, including a sales call, a number of behaviors and consequences occur simultaneously that influence future occurrence but that do not cause the behavior to occur in such simplistic terms as pulling a lever on a machine.

When applying consequences to the field of sales, this means that we have to observe the consequences that salespeople experience during and after the sale. During the sales call, behaviors are changing moment to moment. Salespeople who are not aware of how each behavior is being reinforced, punished, or extinguished lose control of the sale. Effective salespeople alter their performance in the moment to have the desired effect on the customer. They may develop a plan with an outcome in mind, but they also have to observe the customer's behavior to see how their plan is working or not working to ensure that they get the result they want. They observe the effect the plan is having on the behavior of their customers and devise or revise their behavior accordingly to make the interaction more reinforcing to the customer.

The question—what do salespeople want?—could also be rephrased as, what do salespeople find reinforcing? Some salespeople might find selling solo to be reinforcing. Others might find leaving work early reinforcing. Others might find working late or working more flexible hours reinforcing. Some might find it reinforcing to be pioneers on their team or to have solid relationships or fun with their clients. Some salespeople can leverage their need for different kinds of reinforcers into additional sales. Others have not yet figured out the link between their personal reinforcers and their sales success. They might not yet find selling (the way they currently sell anyway) to be fun. They might struggle with the sales process or the product or the service. They might struggle when trying to describe it to others. They might have difficulty overcoming objections or making public presentations. They might view the word *no* as a NIC rather than as a signal for a certain response that could lead to more PICs. In each case, those things that are PICs for them drive their behavior and those that are NICs for them stop or suppress their behavior. Knowing the PICs for one person and the NICs for another is useful when attempting to understand why people do what they currently do and why they do not do what they know they should do.

As a sales coach, you will be most effective when you know the salesperson's reinforcers. One way to identify individual reinforcers is to ask. An efficient way is to develop a list of reinforcers (tangible, social, customer-based, work-based) for each of your salespeople. Salespeople could also begin to apply this method to their customers by developing a list of possible and known customer reinforcers. The Premack Principle can also be applied here to both the selling and coaching process. Coaches should teach salespeople how to apply the Premack Principle to their own behavior. (See chapter 6.)

Coaches might share many of the same reinforcers that their salespeople and customers share. Coaches might be influenced by the same PICs and NICs. Issues of control may be either reinforcing or punishing to coaches, so coaches might drift toward details and micromanagement. Coaches might shift toward more, or less, administrative work (some people seem to like it, while others do not). If someone (a salesperson or sales coach) is really good at administrative work, it could be that he finds this kind of work reinforcing. It might also mean that he finds these other tasks more reinforcing than the primary job. Individuals who struggle with their primary job may find more reinforcers elsewhere (in non-work related activities, in administrative tasks, or in playing politics within the organization). This might suggest that the employee is more naturally suited to other kinds of work.

The Perils of Planning

As experienced sales coaches know, some of the best plans need to be changed on certain sales visits. Successful salespeople read customer cues to determine which behaviors are and are not adding value and shift their plan to best achieve that value. In some cases the plan must be completely abandoned.

Nevertheless, sales coaches sometimes express concern that some of their salespeople take their plans too literally and then jam them down the customer's throat. When customers are forced to just hold on until a presentation is over, they often lose interest in buying. If sales coaches know this, then why don't they prepare their salespeople for such circumstances? Perhaps some plans are too focused on the product and service and less focused on *the customer's needs*. If salespeople begin with determining and addressing the customer's needs and the value that the customer finds in the products, services, or even in the sales visits, they may begin then to build plans that are useful and effective. If salespeople merely plan on reading a spiel, their customers may look as though they are listening but are more often preparing their objections to buying. Salespeople who revert to script reading may benefit more from a less-structured plan that helps them address customer needs and prepare for various customer responses. The challenges of planning might also be caused by a lack of fluency in how to plan. If fluency is an issue, the coach may need to help the salesperson build fluency through more repetition of the right kind of planning over time.

Post-call Analysis as a Prelude to Future Selling

When does the best planning for the next visit with a customer occur? It starts right after the last call a salesperson had with that customer. Right after a call is probably when your salespeople remember most clearly the customer's statements regarding needs, likes, and dislikes. This is also a good time for the salesperson to note the words and actions that seemed reinforcing or punishing to that particular customer. Quick and precise post-call documentation and analysis can help successful salespeople plan better for the next visit with a customer or for other visits with similar customers. Writing a plan for the next visit with a customer immediately after visiting that customer shouldn't be a long process and should save time in the long run. Salespeople can write down the lessons they learned on the call, the customer's needs (stated or probable, present or future), the actions to take on the next call, the questions they might ask, or the product or service they might provide. This kind of post-call work then helps the sales coach determine the best approach for helping the salesperson and, just as importantly, how to reinforce the salesperson for a job well done.

For the sales coaches, the basic structure of the sales plan includes pinpointing leading indicators and results, identifying salesperson behaviors, measuring them, following up, and then checking for impact. In plain language, the steps answer the following questions: What do you want? How would you know if you got it? What are you going to do about it? The next three chapters provide details on each step in the process with specific examples of successful and not-so-successful plans that sales coaches have used in the field.

Key Actions Develop plans that have a point and that are designed for impact on your business. Your plans should help your salespeople have better impact on their customers and their sales results. Precise plans that use behavioral methods as a foundation can be used by coaches and salespeople to reinforce desirable sales behaviors and customer responses.

CHAPTER NINE

WHAT DO YOU WANT?

You can't have everything. Where would you put it?

Stephen Wright

Symptom—Does the sales team act on your recommendations to improve results? Is the information you have read in previous chapters valuable but you just aren't sure how to put it all together?

Remedy—This chapter provides a specific methodology for developing a *predictable* and *repeatable* process to drive results.

I've heard sales coaches boast, "I want it all!" It is a bold, but unrealistic comment. Sales coaches may want it all, but they cannot have it all. Too many of the sales coaches' wants are outside of their control, and therefore coaches are restricted in their ability to develop and implement plans that will help them and their sales staff achieve optimal sales. Wanting it all is also a statement that leaves any sales team clueless about what to do next. I've seen people's desire to appear tough and competitive get in the way of their plans for actually pulling it off. Bragging is not a behavior that makes effective sales coaches or sellers. Bragging and boasting are only antecedents, after all. Joe Namath and Muhammad Ali boasted about their plans, but they were viewed with high regard because they delivered (a consequence) by actually doing what they said they would do—win.

It would be a mistake to view bragging and bold predictions as the reasons why these individuals won so often. Similarly, in the business world, it certainly helps to have confidence and a positive outlook. These are necessary elements of successful coaching and selling. But these are not the primary reasons coaches and salespeople are successful. What happens behind the scenes? What are top salespeople focusing on and planning to do? What are sales coaches focusing on and planning to do?

This chapter is really about how to use the science of behavior change to develop a sales coaching plan that can be precisely and successfully implemented—a plan that has focus, builds in constancy, and ensures for sales coaches and salespeople that the talk matches the walk.

You probably know that you want to win and to increase your sales. I am reminded of a comment a friend of mine, Mike Jeannot, made during the halftime at a recent boy's basketball game. It was a summer league game and only five players showed up (my son and his son made up two-fifths of the team that day). They were behind at halftime by five points and exhausted, since the team didn't have any substitutes. His son Chris came over to get a drink and as he was walking back to the team, Mike wryly commented, "Just win!" Mike then laughed, and I laughed too. Chris shrugged his shoulders. He was tired and so was my son, Alex, and the rest of the team. Chris was probably thinking, Easy for you to say, Dad. He probably knew his dad was mostly joking. Of course, everyone there wanted their team to *just win*. But how do Chris, Alex, and the rest of the team just win? What does the basketball coach do to just win? It isn't enough to say, "Try harder" or "Do a good job" or "You know what to do" or "Just get the job done." There must be specific plans that lead to success.

The team of five did win that game. About midway through the second half our coach switched to a 1-3-1 zone. This confused the other team's point guard, who was unable to move the ball and score against this kind of defense. The coach altered his plan (man-to-man defense) to put his players in a position to win—forcing the other team to turn the ball over and capitalizing on those turnovers. Later, I asked my son what his coach said to the team at halftime. He told me that the coach said, "I know you guys are tired. Keep at it and we'll make some changes to slow them down and get us back on track."

How many sales leaders are faced with similar situations? Someone in leadership stands in front of the entire organization and says that they really need to "step it up this year" and they really need to "fire on all cylinders" and "get excited about this new product." All of that may be fine. It may be necessary in some organizations, but it can't be the only thing that leadership does or says. Leadership must provide specifics about the *how*. They must help the sales force alter the plan or the approach to get more of the right kinds of results. They must follow up after these initial exciting meetings. The first step in this process though is to find those little things that when done will convert motivational phrases and slogans into action.

Gladwell (2000), in his book the *Tipping Point,* provides a variety of examples of small changes that bring about big impact. The

Coaching Plan includes a series of small changes that result in significant changes. But the process here is not just about finding small changes that will bring about big changes. It is also a matter of resisting the urge to change lots of other behaviors that may be important but are not as important now for bringing about immediate behavior change. The following guidelines help determine which behaviors to initially select that have the desired impact on leading indicators and lagging results.

As described earlier, the behavior must be *within the salesperson's control*. The behavior should be *linked with an endurable result* and should *support the organization's strategy*. The salesperson should focus on a behavior that currently has some *room for improvement* rather than a behavior that is already near or at optimal levels. The behavior should be one that has been *proven to consistently bring good results*. One way to determine if a behavior meets this criterion is to ask, "Do the best salespeople do it most of the time and others don't do it well or at all?"

If possible, the behavior should *drag along other behaviors*. A drag-along behavior is one that increases the likelihood that other important behaviors will occur. As mentioned previously, salespeople often want it all and sales coaches often want their salespeople to do it all. Merely wanting it all and having it all are two different things. Wanting it all is easy to do; having it all requires focused work and effort over a long period of time. How about adopting a strategy of getting the results that you ultimately want by focusing on a few things initially? Selecting a drag-along behavior will help you get more of the results you want by first focusing on a few critical actions.

The behaviors of pre-call planning, questioning, and post-call analysis are often intertwined in this way. Selecting one as your area of focus often prompts all three to occur. Selecting pre-call planning as your salesperson's sole focus leads to effective planning on each sales visit. But as your salespeople are planning, it helps to have them do it for reasons other than that their sales coach asked them to do so. For example, planning often involves preparing questions. In the case of repeat customers, if the salesperson has planned the call and asked effective questions during the call, then writing post-call notes will facilitate the next visit with that customer. Many times, I've seen sales coaches pick only one of these activities—planning the call, asking questions, writing focused post-call notes—and after a few weeks, they see an impressive increase in all three behaviors.

I once worked with a sales organization that was making a lot of money. Customers called in and the sales reps sold them a variety of phone services. The initial behavior of interest was *interviewing—asking open-ended questions about the customers' business* as described earlier in the chapter on pinpointing. Most salespeople were not questioning customers in the way they had been trained. In fact, remote call monitoring indicated that the sales reps asked effective questions only about 25 percent of the time. Most of the time, the top sellers asked a lot of closed-ended questions to get quick agreement on the various products and services. The call was fast and they'd get commitments from the customers. Yet, the customers frequently didn't get the services they really wanted and called in to complain after they received their first bill. The salespeople working for the quick sale still had good numbers, but the organization wanted to shift to selling based on customer need which required the sales reps to ask open-ended questions to get the customers talking. The salespeople asked questions about how the customer might be using their existing phone system and then to provide recommendations based on those needs. *Asking questions* became the obsessive focus of this organization as they attempted to improve their selling, service, and efficiency—in a balanced way and all at the same time.

This company had a history of focusing on a thirty-plus item observation form that outlined the recommended call flow. Most of the time, the target items shifted, since all thirty items were important and the organization wanted it all. Sometimes management emphasized the greeting. At other times they emphasized the scripted closing. Sometimes they emphasized professional tone and manner. These items, taken separately, were not the types of behaviors that would drag along other behaviors, but asking effective open-ended questions qualified as a drag-along behavior. The challenge was that questioning the customer, *really questioning the customer,* was harder to do and to track than the opening, closing, and professional tone and manner items on the checklist.

Finally, they began to work relentlessly, constantly, and in a focused way on interviewing skills and noticed that several other behaviors also improved (and they hadn't even focused directly on those other behaviors). The greeting, professional tone and manner, fact finding, recapping, and the closing all improved as questioning improved. When sales leadership asked the salespeople to focus only on questioning and they did, other desirable behaviors followed. Improving the frequency and focus of asking effective questions served to drag along these other important behaviors. The recapping became critical and the closing became easier and more relevant. The salespeople began to know why they were opening (to help identify the customer needs). The salespeople had a business reason to recap (it helped them ask better questions). The salespeople also completed the proper work to earn the right to close by asking effective questions.

Examples of Initial and Revised Plans

The following examples from sales coaches include initial plans and the first revisions to those plans. Each example provides a good start to Step One in the Coaching Plan. First drafts almost always require additional pinpointing. The refinement of the pinpoint usually includes more clearly defining the behavior so that it elicits the desired customer response. You also might have to select and then pinpoint a different behavior if you discover that the initial behavior does not actually drive the key results.

Warning! These are examples of *initial* plans. All include results and behaviors. Some include leading indicators. Simply borrowing the revised examples directly from this text will probably not help you solve your particular sales problem. The plans only became effective in changing behavior when sales coaches did some further pinpointing to help their salespeople focus on the right selling behavior that prompted the right customer responses. *The answer here is **not** found in the examples; it is found in the process of making activities more specific so that they affect customer behaviors and results.* I have provided suggestions and comments after each example to illustrate how further pinpointing might improve each plan. The suggestions listed here do not cover all enhancements and improvements that could be made. They merely describe how to refine the plans so that they are clearer than the initial examples.

EXAMPLE ONE
Pinpointing a Traditional Plan

INITIAL PLAN What Do You Want?	REVISED PLAN What Do You Want?
Result Increase revenue	**Result** Increase in market share for the top 25 targeted customers for product A
Leading Indicator None listed	**Leading Indicator** Customer description of how they might use the product and what their objections are
Behavior Questioning skills	**Behavior** Asking open-ended questions to targeted customers that prompt them to talk about how they might use the product and describe what their objections are

Suggestions and Comments for Example One

The plan described in the left-hand column is sometimes initially developed by sales coaches who either view themselves as already doing this kind of coaching or who want to do it quickly. The example here is really a traditional kind of plan that probably doesn't even require being written down. But for this plan to actually drive behavior change that in fact improves revenue, some further pinpointing is required. Let's start with the result. What kind of revenue will increase? In which part of the business will you see an increase? Which products? Which markets or territories? Once we know the kind of sales we want more of we can begin to identify a pinpointed behavior that will increase the frequency of the desired result.

As discussed previously, the behavior of *questioning* is an effective starting point since it has the potential to drag along other behaviors. But which questions will be useful? When should these questions be asked and to which customers? How often? What kind of guidance is required to help the salesperson listen to the customers' responses and answers? The answers to these questions determine the plan for that salesperson. An example of a better start is provided here. The revenue is from a particular kind of customer and product. The questioning behavior is further pinpointed in terms of what the salesperson is to say and do, with whom, and how often. The leading indicator was not provided in the initial plan but can be used in the revised plan to guide the seller and to ensure that the questions they are asking are having the desired impact.

EXAMPLE TWO
Increasing Call Frequency

INITIAL PLAN What Do You Want?	REVISED PLAN What Do You Want?
Result Increase call frequency	**Result** Incremental increase in revenue from the top 20 product-B targeted customers
Leading Indicator None listed	**Leading Indicator** Time spent with the top 20 product-B targeted customers Top 20 customers' description of the value provided by the product or by the sales call
Behavior Call on all key product-B targeted customers twice monthly	**Behavior** Develop a customized plan for calling on each of the top 20, product-B targeted customers Call on these customers at least monthly Ask each of these customers to describe the value you provided during your call (based on the product or the information you might have shared)

Suggestions and Comments for Example Two

The plan on the left is frequently drafted by sales coaches who are first introduced to this process. It is perceived to be easier to measure than other plans and provides a beginning focus. Historically, many coaching plans are too expansive, so people give up on them after a few weeks. Sales coaches who use this kind of plan may be trying to help improve average or compliance performance—*if they only called on more customers, their sales would improve.* This may be true, but further analysis and pinpointing are required.

The revised plan focuses the result on the top twenty targeted customers for product B. The plan might also benefit from a sales result such as revenue or market share with these focused customers. This plan could benefit from adding a leading indicator such as access or time with these customers. The revised plan adds two leading indicators: time and value. Both time and value have been further pinpointed to focus on specific customers. The salesperson can then observe on a smaller number of calls the impact on amount of time and value with a specific number of clients. The refined pinpoints can help the salesperson not only measure progress but also prompt self-reinforcement.

The behavior of calling on the customer also requires further pinpointing. Three behaviors are listed: planning to sell to each customer, calling on them frequently, and asking a follow-up question to end each call. First, some planning may help guide effective selling during the call rather than just increasing call frequency. Asking a question at the end of the sales call helps provide a frequent quality check for each call.

When plans like these are implemented, they are often revised at later stages to focus on something other than increasing the frequency of contacts. Getting the salesperson to make more calls could be an important change to bring about, but once they are visiting more customers, other behaviors (such as a sales behavior that would help during the call) may become the focus.

EXAMPLE THREE
The Activity Trap

INITIAL PLAN What Do You Want?	REVISED PLAN What Do You Want?
Result Improve needs-based selling	**Result** Increase market share with top 50 customers through needs-based selling
Leading Indicator None listed	**Leading Indicator** Customer description of needs and concerns about our products and services
Behavior Write pre- and post-call notes Prepare a benefit response for identified needs Open your call with a review of identified needs and benefits Share the appropriate sales materials to meet customer needs Ask the customer if the benefit is helpful	**Behavior** Use pre- and post-call notes to develop a specific question about customers' needs such as how they might use the product Ask the customer if the benefit helps identify a specific use for the product

Suggestions and Comments for Example Three

This plan is often drafted when a sales coach knows that something like needs-based selling will improve the salespeople's performance. So they focus strongly on this activity. One of the challenges here is that a drive to increase activity needs to be connected to an enduring business result if it is going to have staying power.

This plan could benefit from adding a revenue-based result (market share, volume). The leading indicator might be specific kinds of information customers share about their needs and concerns.

The behaviors listed here are reasonable, although asking someone to do all of these behaviors on every call will backfire. Asking salespeople to do one or two critical things instead will have a better effect than asking for it all. The method of selecting a drag-along behavior might be the best option here. Select one or two of the behaviors listed that drag along the others. Pre- or post-call notes often drag along other behaviors. You have to plan to do something like open the call, ask a question, observe a customer response, or close the call. You might also make post-call notations about how your questions worked on this call, what the customer agreed to do, the customer's remarks about his or her needs, or the questions you should ask next time.

EXAMPLE FOUR
The Attraction of Closing

INITIAL PLAN What Do You Want?	REVISED PLAN What Do You Want?
Result Number of closes on all products	**Result** Incremental revenue increase in the top 50 customers
Leading Indicator Number of customer yeses to sale	**Leading Indicator** Number of customer agreements to the sale or the next step in the sales process
Behavior Call on targeted customers Increase the use of sales aids during customer visits	**Behavior** Call on the top 50 targeted customers at least once monthly Use sales aids to prompt customers for commitment to the next step in the sales process (to buy, to provide more information, to describe their objections, concerns, or needs)

Suggestions and Comments for Example Four

This plan includes a favorite of many sales coaches and sales leaders—closing or gaining customer commitment. It also includes an ambitious and broad target of increasing the closing on all products. Often when sales coaches select closing as the target of the plans, they discover later that the problem really isn't that of closing; instead, it is a behavior that occurs before closing. Therefore, before focusing on this activity, first make sure that the problem really is that salespeople are not closing enough. (Remember Ken in chapter 7?) Better yet, they may have trouble closing, but some other behaviors like questioning, overcoming objections, product knowledge, listening skills, or identifying customer needs may be required before their actual closing rates will increase in a way that will also result in more sales. You may increase their closing rate, but you also want the increased closing to lead to more sales.

Identify a key result that has a more direct financial impact such as market share or volume. This key result might include number of products per deal or number of requests for additional information.

Customer commitments are really leading indicators and would belong in this category within your plan. If you are certain that a leading indicator should be *increasing customer commitment,* then you should target certain customers, products, or services to narrow the focus. Narrow the focus but expect more rapid impact within that narrow range. Also consider focusing on trial closes or commitments to events other than the final sale such as a request for additional information, agreement to meet again, or agreement to some next step. If the leading indicator is not customer commitment, identify other customer responses and outcomes that might be worth targeting such as more frequent access to customers, more time with customers, or identifying customer needs.

The behavior of calling on more customers is a reasonable first start. It is one of those behaviors that you might refine when contact frequency increases. This example specifies a targeted list of customers, which will help in focusing the sales efforts. *Use of sales aids* could require additional details. What exactly do you want the salesperson to do with the sales aid? Do you want them to read it? Do they need to check in with the customer as they are using it to see if they are getting the desired response? I would recommend that you observe the salesperson to find out what *using sales aids* looks like so that you can help to further pinpoint the behavior you have in mind. Many plans can be improved by focusing specifically on the customer reaction—observing customer behavior during the sales call or asking customers to describe their reactions to the sales aid or sales information during the sales call. Ensuring that feedback is built into the sales process has quickly accelerated hundreds of action plans. Exactly how this is done, of course, must be further pinpointed.

EXAMPLE FIVE
Going After New Business

INITIAL PLAN What Do You Want?	REVISED PLAN What Do You Want?
Result Increase monthly revenue from new sales	**Result** Increase monthly revenue from new sales (annual goal: $300,000, no month below $10,000; shoot for $25,000 each month) Increase in number of product A and B sales
Leading Indicator Increase client contact with a goal of tripling contact from last year Increase the number of client reviews completed	**Leading Indicator** Number of client reviews completed per month where client shares information on product A and B needs, and shares referrals Number of monthly meetings with likely product A and B clients
Behavior Complete client reviews and profiles to uncover opportunities Track client contacts weekly	**Behavior** Conduct 10 client reviews monthly and profile each to uncover opportunities (probing, looking for needs, searching for opportunities, asking for referrals) Track client contacts weekly (outbound phone conversations, face-to-face discussions, mail contact) and share information with your sales coach

115

Suggestions and Comments for Example Five

This plan focuses on increasing a specific kind of sale—new business. Some background may help in interpreting this plan. The result here is to increase year-end performance but it also has built-in subgoals. This particular sales coach was dealing with cyclical performance that was a normal part of the business. In some months, sales exceeded $50,000 in new business alone. In other months there was no new business. The sales coach wanted new business results at a high-and-steady rate. He knew he couldn't do away with the highs and lows, but he wanted higher performance during the low months. This plan was designed to get more high performance through more diligent and consistent work from one of his salespeople.

The result listed here is a good start for this plan. Some other details may help in clarifying the results we are talking about. It is new business, but which kinds of sales would be desirable? Should the new sales include certain products, certain kinds of new customers, referral-based customers, smaller initial sales, larger and longer term sales, and not just calls that come in, but sales opportunities that are uncovered? In the revised example, this sales coach focused on product A and B revenue, acceptable foot-in-the door sales for growing new business.

The leading indicators are also examples of good starts. More detail might be helpful here as well. What kind of customer contact do we desire? Which customers might give us business sooner than the more challenging customers? Completing an annual customer review might be helpful, but what might the salesperson look for as he or she completes the reviews? What kinds of opportunities might be uncovered during the reviews? The intent of the plan is to help the salesperson to be more proactive and not wait for business to come in. How can we help the salesperson be more proactive based on the customer response? The revised plan focuses on doing a certain number of client reviews each month so that the reviews can be spread out throughout the year and will possibly fuel more new business.

The behaviors listed here are often used when attempting to increase sales activity. This can be an effective strategy for helping your sales professionals. The challenge here though is to help your salesperson get beyond mere compliance. One way to do that is to help put the salesperson in touch with some positive customer responses—PICs—that occur early and frequently. The sales coach should focus on providing enough specific detail to the behavioral pinpoints so that good things happen when the salesperson tries the behavior. The sales coach might ask the salesperson to share the best customer reaction they got that week based on one of the reviews that they completed. Another element here is to also check that the salesperson can do a review properly and then use that review to create a sales opportunity.

EXAMPLE SIX
Pre-Call Planning

INITIAL PLAN What Do You Want?	REVISED PLAN What Do You Want?
Result Bring in $500,000 of the total revenue for the department per month	**Result** Number of products per deal per month Monthly revenue per deal (goal: $500,000 per month)
Leading Indicator Number of client calls Number of pre-call meetings	**Leading Indicator** Number of pre-call meetings with targeted list of high impact customers
Behavior Hold more pre-call meetings monthly	**Behavior** Identify and refine the list of targeted customers who are likely to benefit from multiple product sales Conduct two pre-call meetings per week in which you provide details about the necessary elements of a pre-call to optimize the sale

Suggestions and Comments for Example Six

This plan has an important result. This plan could be refined to identify certain kinds of revenue or certain kinds of customers or certain subgoals per month that could keep the salesperson focused. The sales reps could also benefit from focusing on products per deal to help them manage their own activity.

The leading indicators are reasonable starts—increasing calls and pre-call meetings are historically correlated with an increase in sales. Are there any other details that might be added to help salespeople determine if they are getting the right customer reaction? The number of calls and meetings might be adequate, but those requirements might also encourage compliance—*I did this to please my boss rather than to sell more.* If the salesperson is doing this just to please the boss, it is predictable that the salesperson will arrange for easy meetings and easy-to-see contacts (many by phone, many close to their home or office, and calls to friends).

The behavior listed here will be refined over time. Plans that provide some flexibility also help the salesperson get involved in identifying which activities are important and in owning the plan a bit sooner. The behavior of interest here will be further refined as pre-call meetings occur. This is a more inductive approach than the previous plans and is useful to help the salesperson become actively engaged in implementing the plan. This kind of flexible plan is also useful when all essential details aren't yet known.

EXAMPLE SEVEN
Team-Level Plans

INITIAL PLAN What Do You Want?	REVISED PLAN What Do You Want?
Result New assets	**Result** New assets ($2 million per month for Antonio and Dorothy; $1.5 million per month for Carlos, Shari, and Scott; $1 million for Isaac, Franz, and Leigh)
Leading Indicator Number of referrals identified Number of influencers identified Number of client contacts	**Leading Indicator** Number of referrals for products A, B, and C Client suggestions about how to best ask for referrals
Behavior Ask for referrals by using the script Ask clients for their advice on how to ask others for referrals Track best practices for how to ask for referrals and share with your sales coach weekly	**Behavior** Each time you have customer contact, ask clients for their advice on how to ask others for referrals and to identify the specific steps required to do this well Develop and implement your method of asking for referrals based on customer responses Share how you ask for referrals each week with your sales coach

Suggestions and Comments for Example Seven

This plan was initially designed to be rolled out to a team of sales-people. Some sales coaches are hoping to make their coaching lives simpler and develop one Coaching Plan for their entire team. One reason is that it may be easier for them. Another reason is that it provides clarity for the entire team. This focus extends to results, leading indicators, and seller behaviors.

This result seems reasonable. Other details might help the salespeople focus on the right results: can it be *any* kind of new assets or *any* kind of customer? The leading indicators are also frequently used by sales coaches. There may be too many here to provide focus. Pick one for the first month to jump-start the plan. Also provide more details about which kinds of referrals, influencers, or contacts are desired. The behaviors listed here suggest that more details are included outside of the plan. This sales coach had a script. A script can be an effective tool to get started, but should not be used without first testing the customer reaction to the script. Whenever a script is used, encourage the salesperson to observe or listen to the customer response so that they are not just *talking* at the customer. *Asking clients for their advice* is a clever way to prompt clients to provide helpful feedback to the salesperson. Tracking best practices can be helpful if the salespeople can identify best practices and know how to share them. The sales coach might have to ask some thorough questions to identify the best practices. Best practices should be described in an objective way, so that the salespeople know exactly how to replicate them.

Tips for Improving Pinpoints

The examples of "What do you want?" described here provide a starting point for the sales coach. Typically, these beginning plans are revised at least twice to ensure they help achieve the desired impact. The first revision is to the initial draft. The second revision often occurs after the sales coach has a conversation with the salesperson or perhaps has observed the salesperson in action. This phase of revision is to help the sales coach provide clearer expectations to the salesperson. Other revisions may be necessary to refine the plan even further. For example, the behaviors may be described in more specific ways or other customer responses are identified that better link to the desired result. Sometimes the plans are completely revised based on evidence: "We've seen a change in the behavior, but little or no change in the customer response." "The customer is responding differently, but it is not due to the seller behavior." "The behaviors and leading indicators are improving, but for some reason, the results aren't improving."

Changes based on behaviors and customer responses often can be made within the first couple of weeks of implementing the plan. The time frame for evaluating the impact on results varies based on how frequently the results are reported and the lag time between when sales behaviors occur and sales results are generated. This could be almost no time, a few hours, days, weeks, or months. The longer the lag time, the more difficult it is to ensure that behaviors and leading indicators are having the desired effect on results.

Precise pinpointing is not just about adding more details. Precise pinpoints should be specific enough, focused, and include the right mix of behaviors that prompt the right customer responses that lead to the right kinds of results. Here are a few general tips for improving your pinpoints.

1. Write pinpoints that describe and answer the question, what does that look like?

2. Involve your salespeople in pinpointing. Is it an important result for them? Can they describe the desired customer behavior? Are they clear on the desired selling behavior? Can they do it now?

3. Since so many initial plans are extremely ambitious, refine sales plans so that they are attainable and help the salesperson sell better today.

4. Ensure that pinpoints include all essential characteristics: specific, observable, measurable, reliable, linked, controllable, and active.

5. Make the plan more specific and assume it is not specific enough after you develop the first draft (even if you think it is fine). It may be specific enough for you, but will it be specific enough for your salespeople?

6. Ensure the results are strategically important now and later in the year.

7. Narrow the focus to a targeted group of customers, a specific product, or a shorter time period.

> **Key Actions** Develop sales plans that include precise pinpoints that are clear enough to provide useful answers to the question, **what does that look like?** Make sure that you start with a key result, identify indicators from the customer, and then describe a sales behavior that will elicit the desired customer response.

CHAPTER TEN

HOW WOULD YOU KNOW?

You can observe a lot just by watching.

Yogi Berra

Symptom—What evidence do you have that your sales coaching is effective? Does it include more than results? Does it include how customers are responding and how your salespeople are selling?

Remedy—Use joint sales calls and field trips not just to check and inspect but to gather information on the successful work that is happening within your team and also to *reinforce* and *help*.

So you believe you've developed an effective plan. Keep in mind though that a plan that looks good on paper, if not implemented, will only have wasted the time of the sales coach and the salesperson. The point of the sales plan is to help the salesperson focus on important selling behaviors that improve results. How do you know if your sales plan is worthwhile? How do you know if your Coaching Plan is an effective one? How would you know that the Coaching Plan you selected is having the desired impact not only on the results that you want to improve, but on the behaviors and leading indicators that are early signs of success?

You can determine if your plans are successful by examining the *who, what,* and *how* of your plans. The *who* answers the question, who could provide evidence that the plan is having the desired effect? This could be anyone observing the sales process in action: the salesperson, the customer, or the sales coach.

The *what* refers to the elements of the plan that can be tracked. This should include the critical selling behaviors, the leading indicators, as well as the results. The evidence should support the behaviors and results that you identified in the "What do you want?" step described in the previous chapter. This might include quantitative measures (how many, how often, percentages) as well as qualitative measures (more value, better impact).

The *how* refers to the different methods for collecting this information. This might include salesperson self-report/self-tracking, sales coach or peer observation, asking others, and reviewing reports. This also should include measures that capture the impact of sales planning sale-by-sale, daily, or at least weekly. The discussions over time should focus on the *consistency* and *constancy* of the activity. The point here is to focus frequently on the same general behaviors over time. Behavior change requires a frequency of review as well as a constancy of focus on the same kinds of behaviors over time.

Another step of the *how* is to identify existing measurement tools such as sales reports (daily, weekly, or monthly reports), observation forms, and sales process forms. Plans that require the development of additional reports often make the plan more challenging to implement. This doesn't necessarily mean that you should not develop additional tools to help you gather evidence for your coaching impact. Here's a fairly simple rule of thumb: use the tools you currently have to measure your impact and add additional measures if the existing measures do not give you reliable measures frequently enough. Plans that rely solely on monthly reports won't often have the desired impact. Daily or weekly measures offer better information to sales coaches who are attempting to follow trends and provide immediate and certain consequences.

The following guidelines are designed to help you make decisions about frequency:

1. If you don't see changes in behavior after recording at least fourteen data points, you are doing something wrong.

2. If you track behavior every day, then you should see data changes in less than three weeks.

3. If you only measure weekly, you should expect to see data changes in less than four months.

4. If you measure behavior several times a day, you can see data changes in a few days.

Sales coaches should encourage salespeople to use measurement tools that help them track results more frequently or that enable them to track leading indicators and measure their own sales behaviors in a more precise and reliable way. Long forms that require days to complete can become a full-time job for sales professionals. Detailed and laborious pre-call plans or post-call analysis reports that take hours to complete may shift the focus away from effective, precise selling to a focus on detailed administrative tasks that have little to do with selling.

One sales coach related a story about a time when he tried to get his salespeople to provide thorough, detailed, and complete post-call reports. He was interested in reviewing these on a weekly basis. He found that many of his salespeople were cutting out two hours early each day to complete these reports. The salespeople who were most uncomfortable with selling began to excel at this task. They also initially received kudos for the first time from their boss, because their reporting was excellent. They might not have called on the challenging customers that week. They might not have even sold much that week. But they did great paperwork!

Some of the better salespeople on this team did one of two things. They either ignored the boss's request for detailed reports (and turned in substandard reports), or they continued to sell and turned in no reports at all because they viewed it as a waste of time and they knew the organization well enough to know that the urgency of this request would soon pass. Some of the top salespeople didn't see the point of spending so much time on detailed, post-call documentation. They understood that if they had good sales numbers, they didn't need to spend too much time (in some cases, no time) on sales reporting.

Two individuals finally came forward to tell the sales coach what was really happening in the field. Here's what they told him.

- "Many people on the team are stopping sales activity early to write detailed post-call reports. They are selling less than before and they are now spending more time on an activity that isn't as challenging for them—writing detailed reports."

- "Some of the top salespeople don't see the point of the reporting request and are choosing to ignore it. They know the request is temporary and that they will be forgiven if they bring in good numbers. They also believe that you may be grasping at straws, adding barriers to effective selling, and may be out of touch with how you can actually help."

- "Some of the salespeople on the team think that you care more about reporting than selling, since you mainly talk with them about the importance of thorough sales reporting."

The sales coach was grateful that a few people came forward with this information. He really hadn't intended for his salespeople to stop selling early in the workday. He also didn't intend for his best salespeople to ignore him. He not only thought that post-call notation was helpful but that it was also essential for improving his team's sales performance. This wasn't a request to improve administrative work; this was a request to sharpen sales work. When he heard that people were taking two hours each day to write these notes and that some people were selling less as a result, he was naturally concerned. This was not his intention, but he got the behavior that he asked for since he did not pinpoint his request specifically enough. Unfortunately, his request could be interpreted in several different ways.

The sales manager only wanted his team to write very specific and concise notes at the end of each sales visit that would help them sell better the next time. This should have taken no more than five minutes per sales call. His salespeople typically could fit in eight to ten visits per day. He wanted them to write answers to four questions: What did you (the salesperson) do? How did the customer respond? What value did we provide this customer on this visit? What are the follow-up steps for the next visit? Ultimately, the sales coach was only asking for four concise sentences. Instead he got a lot of variance: One group viewed it as a request for a lot of information and an excuse to sell less and write more sales documentation. Another group viewed it as an unnecessary means of micromanagement and as something to be ignored unless your sales results were below goal. Yet another group viewed it as extra work that required them to talk to the boss about how it was not working. When the sales coach clarified his expectations, the salespeople could then write clear and concise post-call notes to help them sell better on future calls. The request to write post-call notes was no longer viewed as merely an administrative task, but as a habit that created better selling behavior and better customer responses.

Field Sales Visits and Joint Sales Calls

In some sales environments, sales coaches in particular conduct field visits or joint sales calls with their direct reports. The point of the visits and joint calls might be to sell to the top customers or to gain an additional viewpoint on how the customer is responding. In some cases these visits are mandated by the company, and sales coaches comply with the field visits just so they can tell their boss that the observation work was done. In many cases these sessions are not helpful to the sales coach or the salesperson. In the best case scenario, field visits and joint calls can be sessions in which sales coaches gather information on customer and seller behavior to help salespeople sell better. This might include having the visiting sales coach assist in the direct selling, but more often it involves observing the salesperson and providing suggestions prior to and after the sale to help advance future sales. Such a session might even include some help during the sales call where the sales coach asks the customer a question, prompts the salesperson to jump in, or gives some other signal to the seller. A value-added field sales visit has two components: 1) a method for gathering customer and seller behavior observations and 2) a follow-up mechanism to reinforce and coach. The topic of *follow-up* is covered in the next two chapters. The focus here is on observing and measuring performance to help improve behaviors and results.

One of the primary ways to measure impact is through behavioral observation. The best salespeople and sales coaches tend to be highly skilled in observing behavior. They can track what they are doing and saying and how others (customers and direct reports) are responding to them. Sales coaches can find out if they are having the desired impact by applying these five steps.

Sales Coaches & Desired Impact

> ### Evaluating Sales Coach Impact
>
> ☐ Track behavior through actual counts.
>
> ☐ Graph the counts and look for trends in behavior.
>
> ☐ Ask salespeople to track their own behavior.
>
> ☐ Ask salespeople to track customer behavior.
>
> ☐ Analyze and review changes in behaviors, leading indicators, and results.

Examples of Measuring the Impact of Coaching

This section provides examples of how some sales coaches have asked their salespeople to measure the impact of their plans. These plans help the sales coaches track the impact of their coaching through changes in the seller behaviors, leading indicators, and results. Measures help sales coaches gather objective information so they know when to provide positive reinforcement for improvement.

How Would You Know?

- The sales coach conducts direct observations during field trips or joint sales visits.

- The sales coach reviews post-call notes that indicate specifics of each call, including customer responses.

- The salesperson provides a weekly update of key needs and benefits identified via voice mail, e-mail, or in person.

- Sales reports reflect an increase in market share, volume, and so on.

- Sales aids/reprints are available during field visits.

- The sales coach reviews pre-call notes during field trips and remotely if available.

- The sales coach asks the sales rep how pre-call planning impacts customers. This puts the sales rep in touch with the natural reinforcers that occur during the sale.

- The sales rep tracks data monthly and faxes the data to the sales coach.

- The sales rep asks customers if they see a change in the sales presentation or service. This option surprises some sales coaches. Depending upon the customer and the industry, this can be a useful method of gathering impact data.

- The sales rep provides two to three highlights from sales calls on voice mail weekly.

Tips to Make Measurement Easy

The following list provides examples of how sales coaches have started to measure the impact of their coaching plans. The options listed here require some refining and just as in the pinpointing section, the first revisions occur after the plan is developed, after the initial meeting with the salesperson, and over time as the plan evolves.

- Salespeople should collect behavior measures daily, weekly, or biweekly. These measures can be shared with the sales coach on a weekly, biweekly, or monthly basis.

- Weekly or biweekly measures tend to be most useful for sales coaches. In some cases, monthly measures are the most practical.

- Easy-to-use and easy-to-gather measures are typically more useful than those that take more time, work, and effort to gather and to use.

- Self-reporting is often a useful, and more often than not, a reliable measurement option.

- Direct observation by the sales coach should be built into the plan even if the observation is infrequent. Direct observation will help the sales coach verify reported information.

Sales coaches and salespeople should see evidence of the impact reflected by behavior measures within a relatively short period of time, a few weeks for example. Measures that extend beyond monthly are not as effective as more frequent measures. As you measure, ensure that your behavioral measures are reliable. Finally, don't use every measure just because the measures are available or the organization has always done it that way.

Tips for Improving Impact

1. Encourage salespeople to track their own behavior each day.

2. Ask salespeople to e-mail or fax data to you for review.

3. Review progress periodically.

4. Give salespeople a chance to tell you about their sales activity and successes.

5. Initiate calls when you see improvement.

> **Key Action** Develop practical measures that link results, leading indicators, and behaviors. Use a mix of self-reporting, direct observation, and existing reports. Place some of the responsibility for these measures on the salespeople. They can call, e-mail, or provide updates to help keep the sales coach informed. Remember the focus: The activity of collecting measures isn't just to know what happened on a sales call. Measures also help salespeople and sales coaches drive sales. Reinforcement is the link between knowing what happened and what drives sales. Therefore, these measures must provide sales coaches opportunities to recognize and reinforce improvement. The goal is to eventually shift focus from sales-coach managed plans to customer- and salesperson-managed plans. Consistent and constant real-time feedback to salespeople benefits not only salespeople but sales coaches who want to put their salespeople in touch with the right kinds of PICs and NICs in the sales environment.

CHAPTER ELEVEN

WHAT ARE YOU GOING TO DO ABOUT IT?

Never confuse movement with action.

Ernest Hemingway

Symptom—Have you tried reinforcement and found that it didn't work for you and it certainly didn't work as quickly as you thought it should?

Remedy—Coach your sales team to improve performance rather than just evaluate standards. This chapter provides specific examples about how to follow up and reinforce in an authentic way that works. This chapter is about the importance of follow up and how effective follow up can be used to help salespeople implement their plans in an effective and sustainable way. This chapter will also describe how leaders and coaches can ensure that their *talk* (a popular antecedent) matches their *walk* (an important consequence).

So if you're a sales coach, you've identified the results you want to influence. I suspect you've selected a financial result. You've probably identified a leading indicator (possibly a customer response) as well as a desired sales behavior, a way to measure the results and the behaviors, and you have included measures that track progress more than monthly. So now what? Perhaps the following example will help clarify one of your most important sales coaching functions.

Max was a senior leader accountable for an organization of 15,000 sales personnel within an even larger company of almost 60,000 employees. After working with him for six months, we reviewed the progress of the salespeople, sales coaches, and sales leaders within his organization. Next we discussed Max's coaching strategies. At this point he realized that not only his salespeople but he, too, needed to change. He admitted that sometimes he really did get in the way, and of course, he needed to stop this. Max started to examine his behavior and its impact on his staff. We also asked him to reward and recognize the accomplishments of his direct reports but also to positively reinforce important efforts within his organization where people were not only selling well, but where large business units were achieving balanced results— that is, not just good sales results, but also good productivity numbers and good customer service numbers. He really wanted good performance in all three; he just didn't know how to do that.

Max resolved to change some things. He was known for pounding his fist, getting people to jump, promising too much, and overstepping his bounds. He was drawn into fixing customer problems. He also was known as a maverick and enjoyed his reputation of being an effective *outsider* within the larger organization. That reputation was very reinforcing to him, even though the associated behaviors sometimes created problems. For example, he occasionally visited different sites and departments within the organization and when talking with people he inadvertently positively reinforced them for complaining. At times, Max got involved in a way that did not help other senior leaders in the organization. Part of

Max's problem was that his reinforcers were about being fast, firm, ahead of the curve, and being viewed as a maverick. Max needed to help his organization in a different way. He needed to very precisely reinforce some activities, to question and challenge other activities, and to be consistent about the behaviors and results that he reinforced.

The point of this description about Max is that sales coaches and sales leaders need to do something differently if they want others to respond to them differently. They need to be clear with the signals and cues that they provide about the behaviors and results that they see as important. They also need to follow up in an effective way that demonstrates constancy and consistency.

The Question of Follow-Up

A large sales corporation invited me to a meeting with the regional directors and the sales vice president. At a hotel a few miles from the US corporate headquarters in a preliminary meeting, I presented the basics of how to coach sales professionals. I heard that one director was familiar with our approach and had integrated some of it into his everyday interactions with his team of division managers. After the preliminary meeting wrap up, I checked into the hotel, since I was participating in some meetings with sales coaches the next day. As I left the front desk, the regional director, who was familiar with the scientific foundation of Precision Coaching, approached me and started talking excitedly about it. He told me that he had participated in a Precision Coaching session a few years earlier and that when using the process he had discovered one useful question that he subsequently used not just in the management of his sales organization, but in his personal life as well. He also said that this one question he learned at the first session was worth the money he spent on the trip, the training, and the time he spent away from his job.

He liked the question so much because it worked. It helped him get good information; but more importantly, it helped him reinforce people when he asked them the question. In the process of asking the question, he shifted his method of reinforcing others from merely a pat on the back to something that was perceived to be meaningful to the individual members of his sales team. They liked it primarily because the question helped them describe their accomplishments and how they achieved them to their boss.

He continued to tell me about this question, the impact of it, and how he used it the day he got back from his first introduction to behavioral science. When he traveled, he usually came home tired, and he didn't listen well to his wife, but when he got back from this session, he tried asking his wife the question to see how it worked. His wife immediately started telling him about how she had rearranged the basement and crawl space in their home. He usually took a misstep in these kinds of situations by not listening well or not acknowledging all of the hard work his wife did. In fact, he confessed that he often would think to himself that he liked the work that she had done, but for some reason the right words didn't come out. This time he asked the follow-up question that he learned would help him with his sales team. What happened both surprised and impressed him. When he asked the question, his wife excitedly started to provide details about how she reorganized this one area in their house and described her plans for the space in the future, sharing all the specifics, and telling him about the things she had accomplished that weekend. It took her about ten minutes to go through it all. Afterward he said that, for the first time in a long time, he felt like her hero instead of her uncaring husband. He listened effectively and he gave his wife her due attention and appreciation. He genuinely recognized her effort as she talked enthusiastically about it all. He confessed, though, that for this to work, he had to actively demonstrate that he was listening.

He quickly recognized that this question had potential, so he started to use it with his sales team. Someone on the team would get good results. The monthly report said so. He managed a remote sales team and couldn't frequently observe his team in the field. He asked the question to his top results-getters and again he was surprised and pleased that he now heard the right details from his sales coaches and salespeople about how they were getting results and how they were managing their customers. The question also opened a forum for his top sales coaches and salespeople to describe how they earned their results. They were legitimate and authentic in their own reinforcement efforts. They described to their boss how their accomplishments were reinforcing—the extra effort, figuring out a challenging situation, effectively dealing with a tough customer. They also talked about how the customers responded. This sales leader, a few levels removed from the real selling activity, was now gaining access to specific, front-line information that he could not tap into before. All of this was possible because he asked one question that got people talking about important behaviors that were, in their opinion, driving the critical results that they earned during the month.

He was amazed at the response to this simple question and shared these examples right after I checked into the hotel. He followed me up in the elevator to tell me more and even got off on my floor and walked with me down the hallway as he finished the story. He told me every detail about that question, all the good things that happened when he asked it, and the good things that happened when his team members asked it.

My temptation was to just tell you the question at the beginning of this anecdote, but I'm not sure it would have given you enough information to see the value of the question. You might have already guessed it. The question that prompts details and that helps the tellers reinforce themselves, share how they were reinforced by the customer, relive the experience again, and that also helps the questioner reinforce the right details is, *how did you do that?*

Let's review:

1. This simple question helps the questioner get details about any accomplishment.

2. The details often include what the salesperson did and how the customer responded.

3. The question helps the questioner experience the event through the eyes of the storyteller. This has been described as useful since so many salespeople work alone and many sales coaches cannot observe all the successful performance going on out there.

4. Another benefit of the question is that salespeople can talk in a way that is reinforcing to them by describing their actions and how they earned good results during a customer interaction or during a time period of attaining good sales results.

5. Importantly, the question prompts self-reinforcement.

6. The question also prompts the teller to describe how the customer responded and perhaps how they reinforced the customer—"Here's what the customer said after the last visit…"

How did you do that? Yes, it's a simple, straightforward question that prompts people to provide details about how they achieved certain impact in their world. It isn't the question that is important here; it is the response that the question *inspires*. Once asked, the question encourages people to talk and, consequently, to reinforce themselves. The question doesn't even need to be asked the same way every time. It can be modified: "What did you do to get that reaction?" "What did you do to earn the sale?" "What are some of the details about how you persuaded the customer to say yes?" For the question to really be of value, though, the questioner must demonstrate genuine interest by really listening and asking effective follow-up questions.

Effective follow-up requires some consistency. It requires asking for and listening to details. Sellers typically have better details about how they sell compared to their bosses' knowledge about how they sell. Effective follow-up also includes precise reinforcement that is perceived to be authentic and helpful. Asking "How did you do that?" helps the sales coach gather details so that the often empty and general "good job" comment is supported by specific details that the seller gives directly to you. The "good job" provided by the sales coach, when said after this kind of question has been answered, is anchored by specific facts rather than based on a hunch. This question helps to take some of the guesswork out of coaching.

Evaluating Standards versus Improving Performance

In a sales coaching situation, two polar opposites pull at the sales coach and the salesperson. One is the need to evaluate the salesperson for compliance and prepare for providing a rating or performance appraisal. The salesperson may interpret selling based on some abstract ideal call that may or may not exist. The tendency to focus on the ideal standards often takes sales coaches off the track of helping salespeople. It shifts salespeople from a customer focus based on current customer needs to some internal evaluation of how the sales call should have gone, often independent of the customer needs and often based on the ultimate result—a sale.

The other option here is coaching with the goal of changing behavior and continually and incrementally improving the selling process. This kind of coaching is based on several elements: the first is customer need; the second is the current developmental focus of the salesperson—what is the salesperson trying to improve or change? The two opposing forces of evaluating and improving behavior are both necessary in organizations. Both are possible but often not at the same time. Precision coaches focus most of their efforts on the *improving behavior* side of the equation when it comes to the moment-to-moment examinations of behavior. They look at trends in their total job occasionally, but it is not the guiding view of their work. They may evaluate trends after two days of selling rather than after each call. They might evaluate their sales professionals' overall job once a month or once a quarter or once or twice a year.

The evaluating standards view of behavior is more closely linked with traditional HR views of organizational performance. It is a necessary tool to use pre-determined standards to evaluate the performance of salespeople and sales coaches. Yet, when the evaluative model is used to guide performance, the model often sets up unattainable and often ever-changing targets for salespeople and sales coaches. The evaluative approach could be based on all the details, steps, and actions that, in general, make up the best sales situation. These standards of the ideal sales call are often introduced during the initial sales training that most employees receive. I've seen some forms that spell out the full and complete job. The number of steps could be anywhere from a handful or up to forty different requirements that some salesperson or sales coach must fulfill to do the job perfectly. When the salespeople are working on changing their own behavior or when the sales coach is attempting to bring focus to coaching, this ideal state often gets in the way of the real progress and the other critical few behaviors (the primary drivers of the sales numbers).

Here's how I've seen this play out. A salesperson is working on improving how he is selling. He decides to work on listening to the customer during a sales visit. Yes, there are other behaviors that the salesperson could work on (pre-call planning, opening, questions, product presentations, overcoming objections, closing, and post-call work), but this person has been focusing on improving listening skills for the next few weeks. On a series of calls, the salesperson has made progress on listening skills. He may not have been listening well for months or even years, but he is finally making progress in listening to customers.

The salesperson invites the sales coach to observe his listening skills. The salesperson still has some things to work on, of course, but for now he is going to focus on listening to the customer and will work on additional behaviors later. The sales coach comes to visit. They review the sales numbers for the day and then go on a few calls. On each of the calls that day, the salesperson does an effective job of listening to his customers. If the sales coach takes the approach of evaluating standards on each call, here's the likely scenario: The salesperson does a great job in the target area, but inevitably misses some of the other behaviors. The salesperson is looking for feedback, and the sales coach will probably give him the classic, "You did a great job listening, BUT you blew the opening."

On the next call, the salesperson might improve the opening, continue to do well on the key listening behaviors, but perhaps closes too quickly. You already know what he hears after the second call: "Once again, you did a great job on listening and your opening was better, BUT you closed too soon." On the next call, the sales rep improves the closing, continues with the listening skills, but misses something else. "You did a great job on closing this time, and you continued with some better work as you listened to the customer, BUT you missed an opportunity to ask an effective follow-up question from the customer to find out what he really needed." And the same demoralizing scene continues.

In each case, the sales coach might have offered supportive positive feedback; however in each case, the positive feedback was followed by "BUT you didn't..." If your highest priority feedback is constructive, then simply provide the constructive feedback in a clear way. If you have both positive and constructive feedback to provide, separate the feedback in time. Provide the positive feedback right after the performance. Provide the constructive feedback later or provide it right before the person has an opportunity to act on your feedback, such as right before the next selling opportunity. One useful tip is to provide the feedback just before the salesperson can apply the information so that he/she can experience good things when trying the new behavior (a favorable customer response). Say something like, "When you walk in there, try this..."

Reinforce the behaviors you intend to reinforce and correct when it is helpful to do so. Provide the positive feedback and constructive feedback at different times. Give positive feedback right away to reinforce the desirable behavior. Provide the constructive feedback right before they are able to do it again so you are able to do two things: help them stop the undesirable behavior and ensure good things happen when they try the desirable behavior. If you need to stop an undesirable behavior immediately, provide the constructive feedback right away. Providing positive feedback and constructive feedback at the same time will dilute the quality and effectiveness of both.

The relationship between the salesperson and the coach should be one in which the salesperson perceives that the sales coach is there to help. If you ask someone to do thirty different things on every customer contact, they are inevitably going to miss at least one or two of those requirements. When a sales coach insists on always pointing out the behaviors that are missing rather than supporting continual improvement, that coach earns the label of *micromanager* or *nitpicker* from his sales team. Focused coaching that is consistent and constant (filled with more PICs for the right things and few NICs) is the type of coaching that will help change behavior in a positive way rather than getting in the way of steady improvement.

The following chart describes the value, purpose, and impact of the two coaching options of evaluating standards versus improving performance. The goal is to make the focus of sales coaching about improving performance rather than just evaluating standards. Both evaluation and improvement are necessary, but frequent follow-up requires an *improving performance* approach rather than an *evaluating standards* approach.

Evaluating Versus Improving

EVALUATING STANDARDS	IMPROVING PERFORMANCE
Based on the ideal sales call	Based on needs of salesperson and customer
Focus is on all items in the ideal process	Focus is on 1-2 key behaviors that have been identified as targets of change
Ensures reps meet minimum requirements	Goal is to reinforce improvement
Requires coverage and review	Requires focused coaching
Frequency—At least twice a year	Frequency—Daily is ideal and weekly is acceptable
Used to meet corporate internal requirements	Used to drive business and respond to external requirements
Sales coach checks boxes (yes or no) with some written comments to justify the check marks	Sales coach observes behavior and uses data to provide focused feedback and shape performance
Based on general requirements	Customized to individual needs
Receiver tends to comments on the "No" boxes	Receiver focuses on the 1-2 key behaviors
Most often used for training problem reps, new reps, or to meet corporate requirements	Focus is on customer impact and driving business results
Value is to determine a quality job	Value is to improve customer relations and sales results
Competency focus	Behavioral focus

Tips for Coaching Success
"What Are You Going To Do About It?"

☐ Provide reinforcement when behaviors are observed during field trips, weekly updates, or joint calls.

☐ Link instant incentive awards to incremental improvements in results.

☐ Ask the question, how did you do that? to get salespeople talking about the good work they've done.

☐ Design field trips to include details of the action plans and focus on behaviors, not just results.

☐ Ask salespeople for feedback on how the plans are impacting sales calls.

☐ Reinforce incremental improvement in behavior.

☐ Reinforce the salesperson's self-report documentation at least weekly.

☐ Identify and provide tangible reinforcers to celebrate significant milestones reached.

☐ Increase awareness of pre-call planning by sharing real-life examples.

☐ Identify and reinforce customers' reactions and behaviors when observing during field visits.

☐ Use weekly feedback sessions to provide consistent reinforcement for improved performance.

☐ Ask the salesperson to share new sales aids with peers at upcoming meetings.

Tips for Coaching Success (continued)
"What Are You Going To Do About It?"

☐ Request that the sales rep share details of new sales aids with the team. Ensure that you offer options (voice mail, e-mail) that are easy for them and for you.

☐ Take a staff member to his or her favorite restaurant for lunch after they engage in the key behavior.

☐ Review sales strategy one-on-one and ensure understanding by asking the salesperson to describe it.

☐ Model or role-play desired behaviors for the next field trip or joint call.

☐ Observe the use of tools and questioning techniques in the field.

☐ Ask for weekly feedback on customer responses to provide opportunities for PICs.

☐ Reward immediately for all improvements and demonstration of desired behaviors.

☐ Share a salesperson's successes with the rest of the team or division. Be sure to check that the salesperson finds public recognition to be reinforcing.

☐ Have the sales rep present his successes at the next company meeting.

These activities are beginning examples of how sales coaches can provide follow up and match their words with their actions. Consistent with the first two steps in the process, revisions are common and occur when the plan is first drafted, after the first meeting with the salesperson, or tweaked based on actual impact as the plan is being implemented.

Follow-Up Basics

Here are additional suggestions for effective follow-up.

Frequency of Feedback

- Provide frequent feedback if you intend to help change and improve performance.

- Daily, weekly, biweekly, and monthly feedback are effective options.

- Generally speaking, the more frequent the feedback, the better.

- Help your salespeople arrange self-feedback as frequently as possible.

Positive Feedback

- Reinforce incremental improvement, especially early in the process.

- Encourage the salesperson to talk about the positive things they *did* so that you can learn the details and reinforce the desirable behaviors.

- Be sure to provide focused feedback on trends in performance and on critical behaviors.

- Provide reinforcement after successful performance.

Constructive Feedback

- When you need to provide constructive feedback, be direct; avoid sugarcoating it. State your observations specifically and objectively and discuss the impact of the sales call on the customer.

- Provide constructive feedback right *before* the salesperson has a chance to apply the feedback. During joint sales calls or field visits, and right before the next call say, "Now try this instead..."

Key Actions If you were to do one thing as a result of reading this book, I'd recommend that you ask your salespeople, "How did you do that?" Ask this question at least five times to see how it works. I am confident that when you ask this question, you will receive a response that encourages you to ask it again. Remember to demonstrate that you are listening and be sure to have enough time to listen. Otherwise, your gesture will appear insincere.

CHAPTER TWELVE

USEFUL SALES COACHING

The road to hell is paved with good intentions.

Attributed to Samuel Johnson

Symptom—Do your salespeople give you a nervous reaction when you tell them you are going to spend some time with them to help? Have you been surprised when your well-intentioned coaching wasn't received well by your sales team?

Remedy—This chapter provides several examples of how you can ensure that your efforts to help your salespeople actually do help.

Michelle, a senior sales leader within a large sales organization, listened to the information about discretionary effort, the ABC model, PICs, NICs, coaching, and selling. She liked what she heard. Then she said, "Okay, let's put this stuff to use to solve a problem that I have." The problem was that Michelle had a teleconference with her entire team of managers at eight o'clock sharp every Monday morning. Michelle hosted the call during which she reviewed the previous week's results and any notable events from the week. Even though Michelle was considered a solid leader in her organization and had a long history of getting results and making things happen, she reported being concerned about her meetings because they weren't getting her the response that she wanted. She actually described the meetings as "painful." She dreaded the calls and she soon learned that everyone else dreaded them too. She also heard through the grapevine that many of the people on the call spent about a half day on Thursday and most of the day on Friday preparing for the Monday morning drill. People who had bad weeks actually spent this time finding data that provided them with excuses they could voice on the call. Effective performers spent time developing reports that they could refer to just in case they were called upon.

I asked Michelle to describe a typical conference call. She said that she did a quick review of the results of the previous week. She'd then call on the person accountable for a particular division's results. If the results were acceptable, she would say something positive and move on to the next person. If the results were below goal, she'd express her concern and ask the person to explain the issues that were impeding results within the division. The person usually offered an explanation backed up by detailed data. They sometimes owned up to the problems and issues, but more often than not, they gave her lengthy explanations that justified their excuses. She also knew that some divisions consistently performed better than others, but could not figure out how they did so. She heard a few things off-line that she liked and asked people to share their best practices with some of their peers. They sometimes did as she asked, but most of the time they chose not to share details of how they got good results. They did not want to share specific information about their performance with their peers since it might take away their edge against their competition—not other organizations, but other individuals within their organization who were competing for the same bonus money based on the organization's yearly rankings.

Those who got acceptable results were often relieved that they didn't have to explain their weekly activity. They were glad they weren't called on or called out. Those who had a rough week didn't enjoy the call, and if they were lucky they could present information that justified their low numbers. Michelle really wanted to turn this situation around. She thought of putting even more pressure on the poorly performing units but now recognized that another more viable option was available to her.

She made one small change that had a huge impact on the call and on how people reacted after the call. She did not make any announcements about her plans for the upcoming Monday teleconference. On Monday morning, she spoke to each person on the call, summarized where they stood on the report that she typically read, and said something like, "Harry, you had a good week last week. It was a challenging week for the company overall, so what I want to know is, how did you do that?" Harry might have been surprised to be asked this kind of question. He might have been hoping that Michelle would tell him that he did a good job and then move on to someone else, but she didn't. Harry might not have even been prepared to answer that question. He might not have known how he did it. Harry might have just gotten lucky and the good results were due to factors beyond his control. Michelle asked each person who had good results the previous week to describe the steps they took that week that accounted for the good results. Sometimes people made up an answer. Sometimes they said that they didn't know, but that they would try to find out. But those people who described the things they did made a difference. These people talked proudly about what they did and how their customers responded. They described some of the things they did that had a major impact on their business.

Consequently, Michelle learned a lot about what was happening in her organization. She also noticed that the information these top performers shared was potentially useful to the poorer performers in the organization. She discovered that other people who were listening to these descriptions were taking notes about how others solved problems similar to their own. The sessions became useful and the time they spent became valuable to many people on the calls. The top performers described the things they did to get good results, and they began to describe these Monday morning calls as reinforcing. The poor performers heard examples of how they might turn around their lackluster results. The average performers heard specific ideas that they could use to become even better at their jobs. Soon, Michelle's team didn't dread the calls anymore. For a few more weeks, some people still prepared for a half day on Thursday and a full day on Friday, but eventually people realized that such extensive preparation wasn't necessary. Michelle had provided an effective forum for her team to emphasize the positive work that was being done.

When Michelle first decided to change the format of the Monday morning conference, she considered telling her team, "Hey, these calls will be different in the future." But she decided against this kind of promise, which would be a weak antecedent anyway based on her history. She didn't only want to prove it to herself; she wanted to prove it to her team so that she could earn their trust. She focused on demonstrating that this was important, rather than merely saying that it was. She wanted her walk to match her talk. After the first positive call, people might have wondered, what happened to Michelle? Was she just in a good mood? Did she just read a new management book? Did she go to a workshop? Did her boss tell her to fix her conference call meetings? They might have done a lot of wondering at first, but over time Michelle shifted their activity of wondering about Michelle's new behavior to talking about the things that they did and how to repeat them more often to get lasting results. Michelle earned this big shift by following up in a positive and helpful way.

Michelle's intentions were good all along. She wanted good results. She wanted a positive culture. She wanted discretionary effort from her sales leaders and sales coaches, but she was not eliciting the outcome that she intended. Once she realized the negative impact she was having on her team, she used behavioral methods to alter how she, as a leader, interacted with her direct reports. She learned how to prompt other sales leaders and sales coaches to share not only their good results but *how* they got good results. This put Michelle in the position to reinforce the best practices in her organization on a weekly basis.

The point of this example is to illustrate how this process starts with an end in mind—a teleconference that helps, a way to increase desirable behaviors across the organization, and a way to hold people accountable for their results. Before Michelle changed her tactics, she managed by using negative reinforcement and punishment. During the new teleconference, Michelle was able to have the impact that she wanted—good results the right way.

Intention versus Impact

Several salespeople I know cringe when they hear that their sales coach wants to *help* them, especially if that help means a visit from the boss to go on sales calls with the salespeople. Some salespeople take their bosses on these so-called milk runs and show them just what they want to see, which might not be a true reflection of their overall performance.

The best sales coaches I've talked to consistently demonstrate three things:

1. They clearly, consistently, and precisely describe what they expect from their salespeople.

2. They can acknowledge incremental improvement in their salespeople so that they can shape their performance over time.

151

3. They provide coaching and feedback to their salespeople that actually helps. This includes positive and constructive feedback.

The top sales coaches do these three things consistently and with constancy of purpose. When I refer to top sales coaches, I am referring to coaches who consistently get good results. Even when they are placed in difficult divisions, they tend to bring in record results for that division. They figure things out to get the most out of all situations, including less than ideal sales territories. They often receive high marks from their salespeople who sometimes describe them as "tough but fair." The salespeople say that these coaches help them and they ask these coaches for guidance and support. They also consistently describe the value that these sales coaches provide over time. These sales coaches not only get results, but they do it through the effective use of positive reinforcement and the precise and purposeful use of constructive feedback and negative reinforcement when they are interested in compliance with certain requests rather than discretionary effort.

When I think of a model sales coach, I think of John Logan, a division manager who focused on helping his salespeople. He was not there to evaluate; he was there to move the process forward. He observed his salespeople during their calls and knew how the customer responded. He didn't just focus on the sales process in the abstract. He focused on the impact of the sales behavior and on his perception of the value provided by his salespeople to their customers. This helped his salespeople provide value to their customers and helped the salespeople see value in the time John spent with them. On one of my visits with John, we rode with one of his better salespeople, and I also met three other salespeople from John's division. Each of them pulled me aside and told me that John was a great sales coach. They went out of their way to tell me this, so I asked them why they thought he was such an effective coach. Almost every one of them answered "I know he is here to help me." He was not out there just doing time or checking to ensure that people were following the rules. John was there to help his salespeople sell better to their customers, to learn more about their customers, and to solve the real problems that salespeople face.

Examples from the Field

I worked with one sales coach, Jim, who had the impression that he was helping his salespeople. He had good intentions to do diligent work for the organization by making sure that his people followed the sales process. After field visits and joint sales calls with his sales force, he provided some of the best documentation I've ever seen. The documentation was detailed, thorough, and neat. Every *t* was crossed and every *i* was dotted. His boss was impressed, and he held up these reports to the rest of the organization saying, "I want all documentation to look like Jim's documentation." Jim was viewed in high regard by the training department too. If you needed some-one to verbally describe how to do the sales manager job, Jim was the person to do it. He could give you specific details about how he coached people and how the sales job should be done.

There were a couple of problems though. Jim's people said that he absolutely drove them crazy. He micromanaged their work and often missed the point of their job duties. He was not there on the joint sales calls and field visits to help them sell better. Jim was there as a patrolman. His job wasn't to catch them doing it right, but to catch them doing it wrong, and he always found the opportunity on every call. No matter how many things the salesperson did right, Jim found the one thing done wrong. He was correct and he was right, but he wasn't helping. His people told him so in a leadership survey, and his people told me the same thing when Jim wasn't there. They said, "He's a nice guy, but he isn't a sales guy. He is more concerned with following the rules and quoting the textbook answers that corporate recommends than he is in doing the right thing by the customer. The customer may be thrilled with the work we are doing, but if we don't do the job strictly according to the corporate sales guidelines, Jim is going to point it out."

Here's the remarkable thing about Jim. He found out what his people really thought about him. He did some soul searching. He intended to help and didn't know that he wasn't helping that much. So he, unlike so many other people in his position, did something about it. He made it his personal goal to improve his time with his people so he really did help. He wasn't about to go out there and tell them, "It's going to be different now; I am here to help," which would be a dubious antecedent. He took a different approach. He knew that only saying he was going to change wouldn't be believable. His people would run the other way if he stated his intention to change. Instead, he knew he needed to demonstrate his intentions with actions rather than with words.

He addressed the problem head-on. He shared some of the specific feedback he had received in a nonjudgmental, nondefensive way with his salespeople. He was candid with his team about his understanding of his past discrepancies. This earned him some credibility. He described his original intentions and, subsequently, made some major corrections during his field visits and joint sales calls. Next, prior to each visit, he sat down with each salesperson and asked for a description of how he might best help during that visit. He indicated that he would still provide an overall evaluation during the visit, but it would be at the end of the visit and the evaluation would be brief. He indicated that he only needed to take this approach once a quarter as preparation for the performance appraisals. He also indicated that he wanted to primarily use the visits to help improve sales. In some cases, he shared specific Coaching Plans that he had drafted. With other salespeople, he acknowledged incremental improvement as he observed it. The improvement might have been in the area of pre-call planning, something that happened during the call such as questioning skills, needs-based selling, listening skills, or actions at the end like post-call documentation. Some of his people wanted to focus on how to best target the right customers. The difference here is that with all of his salespeople, he was asking them to specifically describe *how* he might help.

The most important thing Jim did was to reach an agreement with his salespeople about how they would work together at the beginning of the visit and to ask the value question at the end of the visit. He would ask people if he helped, how he helped, and, if he didn't help, how he might help them in the future. He documented his focus as a sales coach. His salespeople wrote down what they needed from him that would specifically help them during the visits. At the end of the visit, they would evaluate how they each did. Jim provided feedback and reviewed his observations. His salespeople provided feedback about how Jim either helped or did not help. Jim received feedback on his coaching at least two times per week, since he spent at least two days in the field observing his salespeople and doing joint sales calls with them.

Jim began to improve. He began to receive better feedback on his leadership survey and importantly, his salespeople's behavior improved, their impact on their customers improved, and their sales results improved. Jim enjoyed the coaching more. He also didn't sweat every detail on the calls. He said that, at first, it was difficult to change, but that eventually this new approach was a blessed relief. He could focus on the issues that were important rather than slogging through the checklist. His salespeople actually started to enjoy Jim's presence in the field. He was no longer there to catch them doing their jobs wrong; he was there to catch them doing their jobs right. His positive intentions soon matched his impact.

Tom Klein, currently an executive leader with a large sales organization, did something that was both clever and effective when he was managing a team of division managers. His team had strong sales numbers and they were confident in their coaching and their results. Nevertheless, Tom was concerned that they were not working to optimize sales. He was also concerned that some of the top salespeople were getting results today but not necessarily the right way. Based on their current behavior, they would likely struggle with meeting their goals if and when the environment changed (as it inevitably does).

Tom shared an example with his team. He described a top salesperson who had been carrying his division for a few years. He had a couple of big accounts and had won two major sales trips because his results were exceptional. Yet, there was a catch.

When the sales coach visited this top salesperson, he saw plenty of opportunity for improvement. This top salesperson had inherited a great territory and had relied on a few major accounts, but was not doing anything to develop 90 percent of his territory. He had strong relationships with a few key customers, but he hadn't sold them on the true value of the product. When he visited current customers, he would just bump into them, say hello, and see how things were going— nice guy, good numbers.

Tom asked each of his ten division managers how they might handle this situation. They were willing to be honest with Tom. Each person indicated that in the end they would leave well enough alone. Why mess with success? The results are there, so why rock the boat? Each person agreed that they were best served by focusing on other problems and issues on their team.

Tom thanked them for being candid. Then he asked them to consider the scenario again with one change. What if it were one year later and that same salesperson with those same behaviors was not meeting his sales objectives? Now what would they do? The answer came quickly, almost simultaneously: Focus on behaviors as well as results. If you do not, you encourage shortcuts and undesirable behaviors. You also make it more difficult to manage performance.

One of the division managers remarked, "If we don't address the problem today when the results are good, the salesperson tells us, 'I've been doing this work the same way for X number of years and you haven't said a thing. Now that the results are not great, you suddenly have a problem with how I do my work.'" If you provide help and feedback when results are good, you are in a better position to provide feedback when the results are not so good. You also put yourself in a position to improve the results before they start to decline, perhaps avoiding a future drop in results.

Tom's work with his division managers provides an example of how to create the kind of environment in which behavior is looked at—*really* looked at—because focusing on behavior has economic value, not only when results aren't so good, but before the results start to drop. This is a proactive approach, an approach a leader might take to create the right kind of environment for the entire sales team. This is the kind of environment in which a sales coach can help salespeople work through the tough challenges that they inevitably face as they attempt to sell each day. It is a way to help them deal with all those nos they hear, and a way to give them an option for planning to respond to a no in a manner that will advance the sale. It is a way to create, through focused coaching, salespeople who view the no as a challenge, a PIC, as the *beginning* of a sale.

Key Actions Look first at the impact you are having now. Decide the behaviors and results that you want more of and that you can reinforce to have an even better impact. Consider how you might work with your direct reports to help them and how you may have to behave differently to have your intended impact.

- Pinpoint and repeat. Practitioners of this method indicate that this is the most difficult part of the process.

- Ask yourself the question, **what does that look like?** to increase the quality of your pinpoints.

- Be sure to ask your direct reports, **how did you do that?**

- Check whether your good intentions are having the intended effects. Use a precise, systematic sales coaching approach to alter the performance of your direct reports.

Epilogue

When I started writing this book in late 2004, my father had been retired from sales for a few years. About eight months ago, he started to work again . . . in sales. During the first month on the job, one of his co-workers provided some history to him about the largest potential customer in his region—don't bother, he heard, the prospect was off limits and had vowed to never do business with his company ever again. Not surprisingly, that was a familiar prompt for my dad. He soon discovered why his company lost favor with this prospect and started to meet with this prospect to find out firsthand why they were not interested in doing business with his company and to determine their needs. In a few months, he had a new customer and had built in some safeguards to ensure that the customer received the products and services promised. He also makes sure that he follows up frequently to determine if they continue to be satisfied. For Dad, the *no* is still a prompt to action.

I would wish the reader the best of luck as you apply this process, but now you don't have to rely on luck for great sales performance. Even when you hear the word *no,* you now have a plan to improve your performance and that of your salespeople, which means happy customers and optimal sales results.

REFERENCES

Center for Management Research, Cambridge, MA. www.cfmr.com

Daniels, A. C. (1993). *Bringing Out the Best in People.* New York: McGraw-Hill.

Daniels, A. C. (2003). *Other People's Habits.* New York: McGraw-Hill.

Daniels, A. C. & Daniels, J. (2004). *Performance Management: Changing Behavior That Drives Organizational Effectiveness.* (4th ed.) Atlanta: Aubrey Daniels International, Inc.

Daniels, A. C. & Daniels, J. (2005). *The Measure of A Leader.* Atlanta: Aubrey Daniels International, Inc.

Fournies, F. F. (1988). *Why Employees Don't Do What They Are Supposed to Do.* New York: McGraw-Hill.

Gladwell, M. (2000). *The Tipping Point: How Little Things Can Make a Big Difference.* Boston: Little, Brown and Company.

Komaki, J. L. (1998). *Leadership from an Operant Perspective.* London: Routledge.

Lewis, M. (2003). *Moneyball.* New York: Norton.

Skinner, B. F. (1953). *Science and Human Behavior.* New York: The Free Press.

APPENDICES

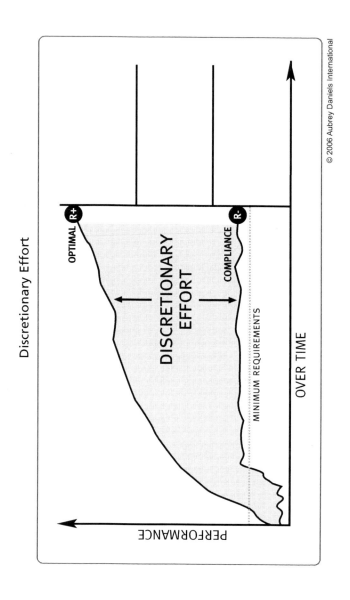

© 2006 Aubrey Daniels International

Coaching Plan

What Do You Want?

PINPOINT

Result:

Leading Indicator: Desired customer response

Behavior: What is the salesperson going to do?

How Would You Know?

MEASURE

Result:

Leading Indicator: Desired customer response

Behavior: What is the salesperson going to do?

What Are You Going To Do About It?

FOLLOW UP

© 2006 Aubrey Daniels International

About ADI

ADI Aubrey Daniels International (ADI) helps the world's leading businesses use the scientifically proven laws of human behavior to promote workplace practices vital to long-term success. By developing strategies that reinforce critical work behaviors, ADI enables clients such as DaimlerChrysler Financial Services, Dollar General, and Blue Cross and Blue Shield, achieve and sustain consistently high levels of performance, building profitable habits™ within their organizations. ADI is led by Dr. Aubrey C. Daniels, the world's foremost authority on behavioral science in the workplace. Headquartered in Atlanta, the firm was founded in 1978.

Other ADI Titles

Measure of a Leader
Aubrey C. Daniels &
James E. Daniels

Ethics at Work
Alice Darnell Lattal
& Ralph W. Clark

Other People's Habits
Aubrey C. Daniels

Bringing Out the Best in People
Aubrey C. Daniels

Performance Management: Changing Behavior That Drives Organizational Effectiveness (4th edition)
Aubrey C. Daniels &
James E. Daniels

For more information call **1.800.223.6191**
or visit our Web site **www.aubreydaniels.com**

Register Your Book

gister your copy of *Precision Selling* and receive exclusive reader
nefits. Visit the Web site below and click on the "Register Your
ok" link at the top of the page. Registration is free.

www.pmanagementpubs.com

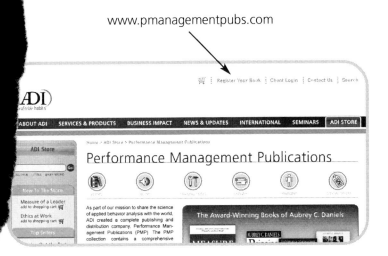